> "Over the years I have discovered that my 'stolen moment'... First, they involve the act of 'stealing' time from our busy lives to enable us to actively engage in fulfilling dreams. Second, they can be those unexpected moments that inadvertently unfold in a meaningful way, enhancing travel ... and so much more. The third context of the 'stolen moment' relates to the first two, in that to make this moment meaningful, its value must be brought to the conscious level and appreciated or celebrated."
>
> — Dennis Stolen

Dedicated to:

My wife and partner Ali, who encouraged me to explore East Africa;

My children (Tammy, Robyn, Dustin);

My mother (Dorothy), and sister (Barbara);

My brother Wayne, who through his living and dying taught us all the value of the 'stolen moment'.

In Appreciation to:

Tasha & Karoma, who so willingly shared their Africa;

My Australian and New Zealand safari mates who enriched the adventure;

NRE Video Productions who gave permission to use the white water rafting photos.

In acknowledgement to:

Ron Olsen, Chief Editor;

Alison Eadie-Stolen, Van Pratt, Peg Sargeant, and Ellen Woodd for their assistance;

My friends and extended family.

Order this book online at www.trafford.com/08-1126
or email orders@trafford.com

Most Trafford titles are also available at major online book retailers.

© Copyright 2009 Written and photographed by Dennis Stolen.
All rights reserved. No part of this publication may be reproduced, stored in a retrieval system, or transmitted, in any form or by any means, electronic, mechanical, photocopying, recording, or otherwise, without the written prior permission of the author.

Note for Librarians: A cataloguing record for this book is available from Library and Archives Canada at www.collectionscanada.ca/amicus/index-e.html

Printed in Victoria, BC, Canada.

ISBN: 978-1-4251-8627-2

We at Trafford believe that it is the responsibility of us all, as both individuals and corporations, to make choices that are environmentally and socially sound. You, in turn, are supporting this responsible conduct each time you purchase a Trafford book, or make use of our publishing services. To find out how you are helping, please visit www.trafford.com/responsiblepublishing.html

Our mission is to efficiently provide the world's finest, most comprehensive book publishing service, enabling every author to experience success. To find out how to publish your book, your way, and have it available worldwide, visit us online at www.trafford.com/10510

www.trafford.com

North America & international
toll-free: 1 888 232 4444 (USA & Canada)
phone: 250 383 6864 ♦ fax: 250 383 6804
email: info@trafford.com

The United Kingdom & Europe
phone: +44 (0)1865 487 395 ♦ local rate: 0845 230 9601
facsimile: +44 (0)1865 481 507 ♦ email: info.uk@trafford.com

10 9 8 7 6 5 4

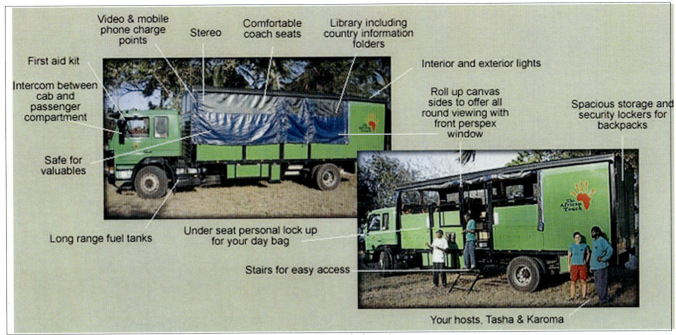
JuJu, the safari truck

Our safari group

www.stolenmomentsadventures.com

Table of Contents

I. **Contemplating A Safari** ... *p.3*
Introduction- A 'Bucket List' Motivation

II. **Getting To Entebbe, Uganda** ... *p.4*
Stolen Moments; London Pride and Kidney Pie; Have You Been Drinking?

III. **In Entebbe** ... *p.7*
Ngamba Chimpanzee Sanctuary; Uganda Education Wildlife Centre

IV. **Traveling Through Uganda** ... *p.10*
A Drive Through Kampala; The Source of the Nile; Jinja; Bujegali Falls; White Water Rafting the Nile

V. **To Eldoret, Kenya** ... *p.19*
A Spectacle for Locals; Crossing the Border; A Blanket Factory; Some Signs of Unrest; The Rift Valley

VI. **At Lake Baringo** ... *p.24*
Crocodile Smiles; Fish Eagles and Hippos, To a Pokot Village

VII. **To Nakuru** ... *p.30*
*Lake Nakuru Game Reserve; Animal Searching;
Busy Baboons, Copulating Cats and Gangly Giraffes;
The Black Rhino*

VIII. **To Lake Naivasha** ... *p.36*
Wandering Hippo; Trekking Naivasha Wildlife Park; Ngondi Village School; Mama Wainaina's Meal; Elsamere- the 'Born Free' Connection

IX. **Onto The Masai Mara** ... *p.41*
*Entering the Game Reserve; First Elephants; The Phantom Hyena;
Visit to a Masai Village; Balloons and Champagne;
More Magic on the Masai Mara (Photos)*

X. **Onto The Outskirts of Nairobi** ... *p.58*
*In the District of Karen; Termite Appetizers; Exasperating e-Mail;
Kuzuri Beads; Hugging Giraffes and Babying Elephants*

... cont'd

XI. **Onto The Ngorongoro Crater Area** ... *p.63*
   A Curdling Scream; Passing Through Arushu; To Kudu Lodge and Campsite;

XII. **Into The Bowels of the Crater** ... *p.66*
   To the Rim; On the Crater Floor; Finding Felines; The Lakes and the River; Leaving Ngorongoro

XIII. **At Arushu Masai Camp** ... *p.72*
   Tanzanite Tales; Visit to the Chemists; Cattle and Camels

XIV. **To The Highlands Of Loshoto** ... *p.77*
   Cameras on Kili; Lofty Loshoto;

XV. **Onto The Indian Ocean** ... *p.83*
   A Long Shortcut to Bagamoya; Lay Down Your Heart; Sunrise Beach; The Luggage Cart to Dar Es Salaam

XVI. **Zanzibar** ... *p.92*
   Sauntering in Stonetown; Kendwa Rocks; Six Masai and a Canadian at Sea

XVII. **The Last Safari Sunset** ... *p.98*
   Conclusion

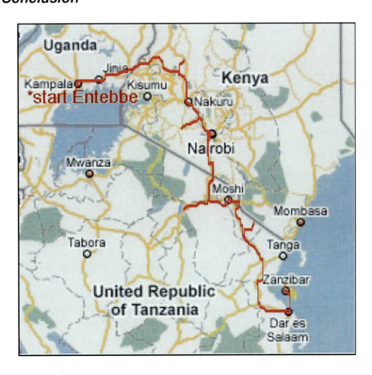

Map of Uganda, Kenya, and Tanzania-Zanzibar safari route

Contemplating A Safari
Introduction- A 'Bucket List' Motivation

The lure of Africa first started as one of those spur of the moment ideas blurted out in my sister's kitchen, "Why don't we climb Mount Kilimanjaro?" After all, spontaneous ideas had often motivated me to experience unique and exciting adventures in the past, and I still reminisced about a number of them: backpacking in Belize; hiking the West Coast Trail in British Columbia; scuba diving in Bonaire; climbing temples in Tikal; jungle trekking across the island of Iriomote in Japan; completing four Ironman triathlons. The process was simple. Think or write down something you really want to do, and go do it before it's too late. It is referred to as the 'bucket list' because originally an item was chosen from a bucket filled with ideas.

Even if you are a person who tends to put impetuous thoughts into action, seldom does everything go as planned. When it was later acknowledged the Kilimanjaro climb would have to be postponed, the original idea transitioned into something else- a real African camping safari. However, I knew that budget would be a major consideration, and any emerging options would have to take this into consideration. Also, in the time frame I had available there would now only be a few weeks for preparation, and in this venture I would be traveling without friends or family. I was fortunate to have the encouragement and support of my partner, Ali.

One morning at coffee a friend mentioned he had a golfing buddy who frequently went to New Zealand to holiday. There his golfing acquaintance had met a man whose daughter (Tasha) had married an African Masai from Kenya (Karoma). Apparently this young couple had met while working for the same safari company. Karoma had already been in the safari business for many years, working for several well-known African safari outfits. With their considerable collective experience, they decided to create their own camping safari business and purchased a new safari truck imported from Sweden. They called their new safari venture, 'The African Touch'.

I found the 'The African Touch' approach unique and appealing in that this safari would intimately explore the Africa in which Karoma grew up, and the Africa Tasha has come to love. This included not only their favourite wildlife reserves in Kenya and Tanzania, but also included the visits they would make to other more remote places many travelers would otherwise not know about, nor have access to. Such travel gems would take me to a remote village of the nomadic Pokot people, escort me to the very Masai village of Karoma's own mother (where she cooks for all a sumptuous, indigenous meal), and tour me to the 'Spice Island' and beaches of Zanzibar. This advertised camping safari would span a month, and would travel over 3,000 kilometres. I was immediately fascinated and knew this type of travel appealed to me.

I was impressed with the contact my friend had given me and equally impressed with the itinerary for 'The African Touch'. As an alternate to the 'Kili' climb (as it is known), this seemed the exact kind of African adventure I was looking for. It was grassroots and much more intimate than many of the other 'tourist- style' safaris I had researched … and most importantly for me … because we were mostly camping, it would be very affordable. I started to make arrangements. I found the two safaris in July and August respectively were already fully booked. However, there was space for me in the June safari if I could arrive in Entebbe, Uganda by June 20th. I completed my registration, booked my flights, had appropriate vaccinations, purchased a new camera and began packing. My hand was eager for 'The African Touch'

Getting To Entebbe, Uganda
*Stolen Moments; London Pride and Kidney Pie;
Have You Been Drinking?*

Stolen Moments
With such a short time to get organized, finding affordable flights became more challenging. In the end I booked a flight with British Airways on line, but it was not the simplest journey. I would fly from Penticton, British Columbia to Vancouver by Air Canada, then connect to a British Airways flight to Entebbe, with a seven and one-half hour layover at Heathrow airport in London. The return trip involving four flights would be even more challenging.

There were other easier travel alternatives, but since I had to make my flight arrangements with only about eight weeks before my departure, these alternatives were all more expensive, and some considerably more so. In Entebbe I was to meet Tasha and Karoma Kimani, and the rest of the safari group from New Zealand and Australia. Although there would be a long stopover in London, I decided my plan would be to relax and go with the flow... to take everything in stride. I would enjoy what I have come to regard as 'stolen moments'.

Over the years I have discovered that my 'stolen moments' reveal themselves in three contexts. First, they involve the act of 'stealing' time from our busy lives to enable us to actively engage in fulfilling dreams. Second, they can be those unexpected moments that inadvertently unfold in a meaningful way, enhancing travel ... and so much more. The third context of the 'stolen moment' relates to the first two, in that to make this moment meaningful, its value must be brought to the conscious level and appreciated or celebrated

All went well with my local flight, and subsequently with British Airways to London. Of course I couldn't sleep as usual when flying, but with my shoes off and two movies selected, I was quite comfortable. It was uncanny that one of the available movies was 'The Bucket List'. Although this philosophy had motivated me to take this adventure, I had not yet seen the film. I found the movie with Morgan Freeman and Jack Nicholson to be very powerful, and felt even more reinforced about my impetuous notion to go on safari. It was then I decided that with such a long layover at Heathrow Airport I would turn the circumstance into an opportunity. I would indulge in one of those 'stolen moments', and add a couple of items to the bucket. First, I would have a pint of real British ale in a typical British pub in London. Second, I would enjoy a traditional steak and kidney pie. I relaxed back in my seat as our plane flew into English skies.

London Pride and Kidney Pie
At the airport I purchased a return ticket to Paddington Station. The Heathrow Express zipped by the typical old brick buildings that are located near the train tracks, and into Paddington. It brought back memories of when I had long ago stayed outside London, and used to travel by train from Loughton into the city.

A few blocks from the station, on what turned out to be a beautiful sunny day, I found an old English pub, just off one of the narrow streets. After considerable debate over which beer, and with some coaching from the bartender, I eventually ordered a pint of London Pride ale. Served at room temperature, the first sip was smooth and satisfying. I took the pint to a sunny table outside and enjoyed London's bustle around me: the double-decker buses; the classic stubby, black cabs; the quaint British shops. After half an hour I set down my empty pint glass and headed to a small kiosk I had previously spotted that sold steak and kidney pie. There is something very unique about the aroma when first breaking into the crust of one of Britain's oldest culinary dishes. As the steam escaped, I inhaled the waft for a lingering minute, then with gusto, consumed my pie.

I still had a bit of time before I had to return to the airport, so I went for a short trek around the Paddington area. I observed how the old classic hotels found off the side streets were tightly crowded up to one another, each hotel door framed by large, white pillars originating from an English era of the past. Next to the station, at the back, I stumbled onto a quaint water canal. The waterway snaked under pedestrian overpasses and disappeared around a bend. Here the canal was lined with numerous colourful houseboats, used as residences. Collectively, they accented a unique piece of English scenery. I continued to saunter up and down small roads and alleyways, and soon it was time to return to the airport. I was satisfied my sojourn into Paddington had indeed been a stolen moment, making my interval most enjoyable.

Canal behind Paddington Station

Have You Been Drinking?
At Heathrow, I casually reported to the preliminary security check to continue my second leg of travel to Entebbe. Everything had been going so well, and I was still exhilarated from my stimulating London interlude. At the security gate, a young female attendant looked at my ticket, as I inquired if this was the correct gate for the flight indicated. She looked straight at me ... looked at my ticket ... looked at me again. Then to my surprise she asked, "Have you had anything to drink?". Taken back somewhat by her question, I told her that I just returned from an excursion to Paddington Station, where over a couple of hours ago I enjoyed a wonderful pint of London Pride ale and savoured a traditional steak and kidney pie.

"I can smell the alcohol on your breath", she replied, and then told me I was not to consume any more alcohol until I was once again checked at the boarding gate. I was dumbfounded by all of this, knowing the one pint to be moderate in terms of alcohol consumption. However, I did not want to jeopardize being able to board the plane and told her I would follow her instructions explicitly. There was still about an hour and a half before I needed to report to boarding security, so I spent the time wandering around the inside security portion of Terminal 4, poking into shops, doing some quick e-mail, and giving occasional glances to those who were seated in the numerous small bars, enjoying a drink before their flight. Soon it was time to board.

The female at the computer was very pleasant and smiled as she took my ticket and entered the code. I watched her face ... it changed. She looked at the computer screen again, and in a pleasant English accent remarked, "Mr. Stolen, would you be so kind as to present yourself to the attendant over there". She pointed to a man at another computer. "He will give you further instructions regarding your boarding."

It obviously wasn't a question. I wandered over to where a young official-looking man in a British Airways uniform was busy attending to the monitor.

"Can I help you?" he asked.
"I was asked to report to you," I confessed.
"Why?" he inquired, looking genuinely confused.
"I think I am being monitored for alcohol consumption," I replied calmly, a bit red-faced. I quickly explained what had happened.

His reaction was one of surprise, and I felt relieved when he smiled and said, "Mate, you seem disgustingly sober to me. Have a good trip, and tell the flight attendant on board to give you an extra complimentary drink on British Airways."

I felt vindicated. Even as I advanced down the loading ramp to the plane, I had already decided it would be a glass of red wine with my flight meal. In fact, with the complimentary drink on British airways, it would be two glasses of wine.

As the plane descended into Entebbe, I could see the lush green landscape below. Open spaces were spotted with randomly planted banana trees stretching along the visible shoreline of Lake Victoria. A sheen of morning sunshine reflected off the lake and caused the water to sparkle. I felt the familiar bump of wheels touching the tarmac as we touched down. Inside the airport, I quickly found the counter to arrange my entry visa at a cost of $50 American. My safari guides, Tasha and Karoma, were there to meet me with their little son, Tembo, and I felt excited when I heard, "Karibu... Welcome to Africa".

Road from the airport into Entebbe

In Entebbe
Ngamba Chimpanzee Sanctuary; Uganda Education Wildlife Centre

Safari Day 1

Entebbe itself is not large, and spreads sparsely along about three or four kilometers of a main road that ascends up to a few streets of shops at the far end of town. Smaller, red dirt roads lined with vegetation branch off the main road. On these branch streets, such as along Church Street, one finds smaller bed and breakfast hotels mixed in with private residences that are adorned with lush gardens and banana tree groves. Tasha and Karoma Kimani transported me from the airport to our first night's accommodation at the Central Inn Bed and Breakfast, where I could relax after the long journey. However, having some free time before the others on the safari arrived, I was keen to explore the area on my own, and set off for a walk. Three hours was sufficient time to view most of Entebbe proper from near the airport, up to the main village on the hill.

For lunch I slipped into an outdoor bakery and coffee restaurant called Smileys. In the patio backyard setting, I was served Ugandan coffee that came with its own small second container of hot milk. I was the only person sitting in the warm sun, and enjoyed friendly conversation with my Ugandan waiter who told me his Christian name was David. I then found out most East Africans have two names, a Christian name and an African name, but most seem to prefer to introduce themselves, at least to westerners, by their Christian name.

At four o'clock in the afternoon my safari companions from New Zealand and Australia arrived from the airport. A short time later I found myself with these new acquaintances, sampling my first Ugandan beer, called 'Nile', and my first Kenyan beer, called 'Tusker'. From the very beginning I knew I was going to enjoy each and every one of these new mates (to which they referred to themselves), and teased that I liked hearing their respective accents, particularly when they said, "Eh mate ... want another beer?" I jokingly informed them that, in some contexts, I was quick to learn a second language. They were as quick to inform me that I was to be their token North American on safari. I was no doubt outnumbered, if not outwitted, by this group from 'down under'.

Lunch at Smileys

Entebbe Side Street

Ngamba Chimpanzee Sanctuary
The breakfast at the Central Inn consisted of several varieties of fresh tropical fruit, eggs, sausages, toast and of course Ugandan coffee with hot milk. With this ample start to the day, we first underwent a safari truck orientation to become familiar with what, in part, would be our new home for the next 28 days. Tasha and Karoma have cleverly designed and outfitted their safari truck to provide for intimate, close encounters with the African wildlife in a safe and secure environment. The vehicle also has built-in personal storage lockers, as well as areas for the general storage for essentials such as food, water and such equipment as is required for camping and other necessities unique to a safari.

With the orientation complete, we boarded the safari truck (named *JuJu*, meaning 'black magic' in Swahili), and set off for our very first expedition. *JuJu* transported us to a boat launch on Lake Victoria where we were shuttled to Ngamba Island to visit a special chimpanzee reserve. The camp consists primarily of a few buildings including a small outdoor lecture centre, a souvenir and coffee shop, tent accommodation for the staff, and a series of raised platforms from which one can observe the chimps in their natural environment. We were greeted with a complimentary cup of Ugandan tea and told about the importance of this special refugee project for the chimps. As well as for the tourists who help fund the project, the platform during the feeding also allows an opportunity for scientists and volunteers to study chimp behaviour in the relatively uncontrived setting. The guide informed us that 95% of the 100-acre island is jungle. Our group was then escorted along the elevated wooden walkway, which extended for some distance at the edge of the jungle area. This eventually led to a somewhat higher wooden observation tower.

As we walked the platform, we saw that a large tribe of chimps of various sizes and ages had gathered at the jungle's edge, and were very noisily complaining that one of their six feeds of the day was late. What they didn't know was that this feeding was prearranged for our benefit, and we were the ones slightly behind time. It was not unlike seeing a bunch of young children having tantrums. Some howled and screamed loudly, others threw their arms around while jumping up and down. However, when chunks of various varieties of fruit were tossed to them from our platform, they settled down.

It was fascinating to watch the antics of the feeding chimps, and to attempt to capture some of their amazing gestures and behaviours on camera. Although reflecting on the uniqueness and intelligence of the species, while photographing it struck me that many of these behaviours were not unfamiliar. Then suddenly, with the feeding at an end, the chimps quietly slipped back into the profuse jungle from which they had come. This jungle, however, was only their adopted home. For the most part, these chimps are survivors from other areas where they had become victims. They may have been targets for bush meat, have been trapped in snares and intended for pets, or have befallen some similar catastrophe. At this chimp reserve, they are carefully healed and reintegrated into a more normal chimp society. The renowned Jane Goodall is a well-known supporter and patron of this project, and the staff was very excited that she was going to be at a fundraiser in Entebbe in about a week, and would be visiting Ngamba. I learned that the Jane Goodall Institute is situated in Entebbe itself. When we returned from the island, an attractive buffet lunch that had been prepared for us was spread out on a camp table. It was our first camp safari lunch, and the view in the park-like setting of expansive Lake Victoria was a wonderful hint to what lay ahead.

Uganda Education Wildlife Centre
After lunch, it was only a short trek to where we wandered through the Uganda Education Wildlife Centre. The centre is as much an opportunity for Ugandans, particularly students, to view some of their own indigenous African animals that otherwise they would not get the opportunity to see. This could, in part, be related to the fact that Uganda has depleted much of its own wildlife, such as the rhino. Although enclosed by fences, in this setting we were are able to view bushbucks, two rhinos, a tribe of chimps, various exotic birds including the shoe-billed crane, wart hogs, crocodiles and a variety of enclosed snakes. The centre was a nice warm-up for us to viewing African wildlife. However, we knew this was only the appetizer to what was to come when we traveled to the heart of the untamed game reserves and parks we were scheduled to visit. What was also wonderful to discover was the incredibly vast knowledge our safari guide, Karoma, had about Africa and its animals. As we casually wandered through the wildlife centre as a group, he imparted this knowledge to us with both ease and humour. It was obvious, even at this point, that he was going to be an invaluable resource on our safari.

Leaving the Education Centre we made our way back to *JuJu* and on to our first campsite of the trip, located in the grounds at a backpacker's hostel and campground just down the road from our first stay. It was an opportunity to practice the camping skills we would need for most of the rest of the safari. On this occasion, however, our tents were already set up, as were the camp tables and folding camp chairs. On a glowing, hot charcoal bed bubbled a steaming stew. Its aroma and taste hinted at many sumptuous meals to come. Tomorrow would be an early start toward the capital city of Kampala, and after a very full first day we were in our tents early for the needed rest.

Traveling Through Uganda
A Drive Through Kampala; The Source of the Nile; Jinja;
Bujegali Falls; White Water Rafting the Nile

Safari Days 2-3

A Drive Through Kampala

During the night I heard the occasional tent zipper opening or closing. I assumed the various times of these sounds were due to our different bladder demands, most likely also related to the various time zones from which we had each traveled. I came to label this late night tent sound as the 'kidney zipper song', and its melody was frequently heard intermittently during the early hours of the 21 days or so of camping on our 28 day safari. I finally arose at 5:20 in the morning, and rich Ugandan coffee was already heating on the grill over the glowing charcoal. After our group had breakfast, we boarded our safari truck *JuJu* and set off for the Ugandan capital of Kampala.

Seated comfortably, and with the side-flaps of the truck open, the ride was both breezy and fascinating. Along the way we were exposed directly to the din, colour and smells of Africa. The roadside was crowded with countless small brick hovels and similar buildings, attached in long rows. In dusty doorways, or in front of the buildings, commerce of every conceivable variety was carried on. Iron gates made from recycled metal were being handcrafted to the sound of pounding hammers and sparking grinders. Tiny phone-call kiosks, some just clapboard stands, appeared everywhere. It seemed anything that might make a shilling became a business. Scooters and bicycles were piled outdoors. Stacked slabs of slate were displayed in dirt. There were fruit and vegetable stalls, open-air butcher shops, hair braiding tables, small bars, cooking tables, and various small grocery items assembled in any possible space. Juxtaposed with all this was the background of lush banana trees and other green vegetation spreading from behind the hovels, and up to hilly regions.

You could tell we were nearing Kampala as the intensity of the markets increased. Extremely poorer sections could be seen, and crowded among them, Ugandans sat in doorways or milled around in front. The spectacle was truly a colourful and rich experience, especially when viewed from our open safari truck. As we passed by, onlookers stared curiously, or smiled, or waved or even yelled out greetings like "Karibu mzungu" (welcome white man).

The actual city centre of Kampala, though not large, was more modern with bigger engineered buildings such as banks and hotels. The chaotic market environment was less obvious here, as we quickly drove through the downtown area and to the outskirts on the other side of the city. Here we made a brief stop at a more western-style super market. We were prudently advised that we might wish to purchase our own toilet paper, just as a back up for some of the campsites that were on our safari itinerary. Some of us were also pleased to find that the supermarket sold beer and wine, and added those items to our own personal shopping inventories. Fully supplied, we set off again into the more rural Ugandan countryside. We were heading to a place called 'The Source of the Nile'.

Outskirts of Kampala

Source of the Nile

Leaving Kampala, we repeatedly passed through various villages. Between villages, there were stretches of sugar cane fields, hilly patches of vegetation, cultivated plots of land, and even a view of our first tea plantation. Eventually we came upon a site where a modest sized hydroelectric damn was situated. Turning off the main road and traveling for about twenty minutes, we arrived at the place where a relatively small river begins to flow from Lake Victoria to begin its long journey north to the Mediterranean Sea. We had arrived at the source of the Nile. Although it was time for lunch, I was consumed with the significance of being in a shady park on a beautiful, warm sunny day and actually overlooking this river that I had studied in grade seven Social Studies. I was really at the source of the Nile. It was a moment to be savoured, and worthy of some quiet contemplation. Over lunch, I reflected on that significance while gazing at the river below. Then, satisfied the moment received the attention it deserved, I rejoined our safari group as we descended the steep stairs to the canopied boats that would take us onto the river, and onto Lake Victoria to the very place where it began to transform into the Nile.

The boat we boarded was a long riverboat with the traditional African canopy, similar to those often seen in the classic African adventure movies. Passing a small rocky island sparsely treed, but overpopulated by crowds of black cormorants, white egrets and a multitude of other birds, we meandered in and out of the adjoined river and lake shoreline. Frequently we would pass natives in their wooden dugouts, as they tossed single lines or nets for the local tilapia fish. We floated by an upper village and looked on a large charred area where local villagers burned saplings to make charcoal. Then we cruised around the area where the Nile actually began, as if to imprint its specific location. Eventually leaving the boats, the finale to our excursion allowed us to ponder a special monument commemorating Gandhi's significant contribution and love for Africa, and honouring his request to have some of his ashes spread at the source of the Nile.

We re-boarded *Juju* to continue on to the village of Jinja, then to nearby Bujegali Falls which is renowned for both its beauty and its extreme white water rafting. En route we passed small villages of crowded mud-thatched huts or homemade brick hovels. The rich red ochre-coloured soil appeared as paint on an African canvas. Its terra cotta dust, which covered all vegetation and buildings located anywhere near the side of the road, made it seem as if everything had been spray-painted. The thick film of red dust was sharply contrasted with the verdant, lush growth a short distance from the road, creating an almost surreal appearance to the landscape.

Source of the Nile

Bujegali Falls

The arrival at our campsite in Bujegali Falls unveiled a wondrous scene. Below the campsite you at first heard, then at closer range, saw the Nile as it formed into rapids, then into smaller falls as the river forced its large volume of water through two narrower channels. The scene from the steep bank rendered a very picturesque view of not only the rapids and falls, but also of the lush vegetation and hilly landscape on the opposite side of the river. At the campsite, on top of the bank, is perched a modest-sized, open-air bar that features a large outdoor deck looking onto the spectacular panorama below.

I was grateful for the two days in this location, but the immediate focus was on exploring the surrounding area. Descending the multiple flights of stairs near the rapids below, with wild abandon a few from our group jumped off the rocky shelf into a circulating bay of comfortably warm water. Taking care not to go too far into the central current of the river, I found I could traverse the small bay and enjoy the return swim in a reverse eddy that propelled me back to the starting area. After our swim, there was an opportunity to do some bits of laundry. Before long it was time to join the group for our evening meal, and I realized how hungry I was. I was told that the evening menu was to be whole-baked tilapia fish that our camp attendants, John and Nick, had been busy preparing.

The wonderful meal of local tilapia rendered this experience very special. After a fairly long day of traveling, I could not have wished to be banqueting in a more beautiful outdoor setting. It also only seemed fitting that such an indigenous meal should be complimented by another local product bearing a most appropriate name for the area, a Ugandan 'Nile' beer. That evening in the tent, with the gentle swishing music of the Bujegali Falls in the distance below, it was easy to drift off to sleep. I knew that the morning would bring with it new excitement, when a group of four of us from the safari would join others to challenge some of the white water rapids that were interspersed along a 30 kilometre stretch of the Nile . It included Bujegali Falls, directly below us.

Bujegali Falls

White Water Rafting The Nile: Razorback Rapids; The Waterfall; Roaring Thunder Rapids

In the morning, our group of four from 'The African Touch' joined other international travelers in the back of an open shuttle truck. We were being transported to the starting point where the rafts would be launched into the Nile. Eventually four separate rafts slipped into the historic waters, and each group began an intense orientation of the skills required to white water raft. This included understanding the concept of the teamwork required to navigate the 30 kilometres, with multiple rapids ranging from grade 3 to grade 5 in difficulty. We began to become aware that this adventure was going to be far more challenging than we had first anticipated, and became very attentive to Mike, our boat captain. We practiced assuming various body positions for shooting the rapids, and responding to Mike's various commands. Then we practiced tipping the raft, trying to stay with the raft when it rolled over, and repeatedly struggled to get back into the raft. Finally, with much trial and error, and some recognized hilarity at our more feeble efforts, we launched with our boat captain Mike.

Right from the beginning the scenery along our floating trip was fabulous, and excitement grew as we sequenced successfully through the first series of rapids of lower-grade difficulty. Mike reminded us, however, that much more challenging rapids awaited us. Our elation was somewhat understandable. We repeatedly observed the other three rafts overturning and spilling out its rafters, while on the other hand we were able to navigate upright through these early series of rapids. We began to feel we were gelling as a team. We celebrated each success with a team 'high five' by reaching in and clicking our paddle blades above our heads. That we were all significantly older than the other eight-man teams, made each successful run that much sweeter.

Scattered between the rapid areas along the route are stretches of quiet waters, which required us to paddle for some distance. From time to time we would pass wooden dugouts with one or two men fishing. Cormorants, king fishers, egrets and the occasional large fish eagle, with its wings spread and gliding in for its catch, became part of the landscape. Women, solitary or in groups and with children, could intermittently be seen doing laundry by hand along the shoreline. On these quiet stretches of water, we alternately paddled, floated, rested, paddled again... all the while enjoying the scenery as it quietly slipped by. Eventually we approached the next rapid, and here Mike stopped us to review the series of commands and skills that would be needed to specifically run it ... hopefully upright. We were told what our strategy would be, and set off.

Rafting Photos With Permission of NRE Video Productions

The Razorback Rapids

We could tell that these rapids had increased in difficulty. In this new current, our raft integrated with the faster flowing, frothy water which could be seen simultaneously falling, rising and coming at us in walls and folds. Water was coming from everywhere. Above the thunderous sound we could hear Mike yelling out the navigational commands: "Forward paddle"... "Down"... "Hang on"... "Stop paddling".... "Lean in"... "Get down", whatever the split-second circumstance required. The commands changed instantly, but unfortunately it took five seconds for us to respond, and on the Razorback this meant inevitable catastrophe. The physical responses continued to fall behind the commands. Suddenly, and seemingly out of nowhere, a gigantic fold of water appeared above us ... and it happened. In order to remain with the raft in case of a spill, one of the techniques that we had at first practiced was to duck under the raft as it turns over, while simultaneously grabbing onto a side-rope. However, what seemed methodical and do-able during practice, was lost in the instant of reality. In a flash, the raft was over and the smashing force of the angry turbulence had torn me away from both the raft and the side-rope. In a split second I was sucked under in the raging torrent of froth, with no time to take a larger breath before being submerged.

We had been told that when totally helpless with the weight and force of water on top of us, not to struggle but rather to lay back with feet up, try to relax, and let the lifejacket do its job. Apparently one would eventually pop to the surface. I fought not to panic, but my tossing body was caught in Razorback's grip and my lungs began to ache, then burn, then feel as if they were on fire, as I fought the now desperate urge to inhale. An element of fear had crept in as I knew I was reaching my limit. I might not make the surface in time. Time seemed suspended, as I thought about my family, my children, my young grandson. Then, faintly, I heard Mike's instructive echo in my mind, "Lay back" ... "Feet up" ... "Wait". I waited .... waited ... waited.

Just when my watery demise seemed imminent, I miraculously popped up. Above the thunder of Razorback I heard my own loud, desperate gasp for air, but all I seemed to inhale was the Nile. I fought for my second life-giving breath, but just as I inhaled, my helplessly floating body zipped into another part of the rapid. Pulled under again, I continued to cough and sputter beneath the surface while being uncontrollably tossed around. I knew I was once again in serious difficulty, but with the troughs of water being somewhat less here, I bobbed to the surface more quickly this time. This process repeated itself again and again. Although continuing to choke and gasp, I realized I had to be satisfied with these small, sharp, intermittent sucks of oxygen to sustain me until the next rise to the surface. And so it went. Though no doubt but a short time, this ordeal seemed endless. Then for a minute I felt some reprieve as I saw a bobbing rescue kayak appearing and disappearing in the rise and fall of the rapids. Swirling around in the still churning water, I also noticed however that he already had another body clinging onto the bow. Fortunately the kayaker realized I too was in difficulty, and he slowly began bouncing toward me. "Grab the back hook," he yelled above the thunder. With both of us clinging onto each end, the short river kayak then began ploughing its way through the angry swirls of water to the nearest raft.

When we finally arrived at the raft, we discovered it could only take one more body on board. They immediately dragged the half-drowned passenger off the bow. I would now have to be towed back through the rapids to my own raft, which by now Mike had managed to turn upright and was busy collecting our remaining crew. Because the kayak could not navigate with my weight at its stern, in my bulky life jacket I would first have to clumsily swim around to the now-vacant bow and grab the front strap. To avoid the drag, I would then have to wrap my legs around the front of the kayak, with my back to the water. In my fatigue, it was a major feat to finally be able to position myself. I was thus plunged, bobbed and swirled again across the rapids to be pulled into the raft by my raft mates. I had no energy left to assist, feeling more spent than after finishing any one of my most grueling Ironman triathlon races. I was hauled in like a lifeless fish that had fought to the bitter end, but now willingly surrendered to its fate. But unlike the fish, I was grateful, even surprised, that I was being returned to a dry environment with sweet air to breathe. Regaining some strength, I discovered one of our team was missing from the raft. After my ordeal, and speculating what could have happened, I became concerned. But I was relieved to hear that although he had suffered a similar experience, he had earlier been picked up by another raft and would be returned shortly.

Rafting Photos With Permission of NRE Video Productions

Finally reunited, we were all obviously somewhat rattled by what we had just experienced. It had all happened in such a short period of time: the strength, power and force of the rapids; the instant overturn of the raft; the total helplessness in the water, as if being submerged in a violent washing machine. The good fortune to be back in the raft became an acknowledged emotion. We were all relieved, but now all equally apprehensive of what lay ahead, especially because Mike then informed us that our next challenge would be to descend over a short waterfall and into some troughs of water that waited below. This collective feeling of apprehension was enhanced when we were told we were only halfway through our journey. Mike also shared with us that sometime previously a rafter had been sucked under the water in the same place where we had overturned, but was held submerged. When he reappeared, he had to be evacuated to a hospital to have the water pumped from his lungs. We just stared at one another, and wondered what else Mike hadn't told us.

Continuing our rafting sojourn, we successfully navigated through the next three lower grade rapids in succession. Once again our team became elated at our success. Other rafts were still overturning, and we began to regain our confidence. By now we were nearing the waterfall, and Mike presented us with the choice of taking an easier, lower-grade line through the rapids, or attempting the more difficult descent over the short waterfall and through the churning troughs below. Somewhat feigning bravery, we responded, "Let's do it!", but somehow the response seemed to lack some of its conviction since our spill at Razorback.

The Waterfall

We eventually entered a quiet part of the Nile, almost a lake, that gave us a bit of repose before we would begin our approach to the waterfall at the far end. Here the safety raft delivered fresh cut wedges of succulent pineapple and cookies. For those so inclined, it was also an opportunity to jump, dive or somersault off the raft, or just to lower the paddles and rest in the sun, leaning against the raft walls. It also was a time to reflect on the wonderful adventure so far, including our spectacular tip and survival on Razorback. Then began a hard paddle across the water to position ourselves to begin, in sequence, a run to the waterfall where we would navigate the ninety-degree drop, and continue into the rapids below.

We finally arrived at the far shore where all rafts stopped. Here we would wait in turn until the preceding raft went over the falls, through the troughs below, and into a back eddy where the raft could rest until all had gone through. The adrenaline began to rush in anticipation of our turn, and the tension and excitement grew.

The first raft went. It overturned, signaling what might be to come for the rest of us. The second raft went, but although remaining upright, it got held at the bottom in the falling water, and a line had to be thrown to pull it out of its spraying grip. The third raft went. Its tip was dramatic, scattering its orange, puffy life-jacketed passengers all over the water below. To add to the drama, in the manner of a stuntman from a movie, the raft-boat captain athletically slid up the rubber side of the overturning raft, and triumphantly stood on its bottom while the overturned boat swirled in the water, his arms raised in victory at not being thrown. Now it was our turn.

Mike had informed us our strategy would be to approach the edge of the waterfall sideways, controlling our speed by his paddle on the shelf of rocks that lined it. From there we would make a controlled spill, sideways, over the edge to maximize the raft's flotation-surface when it hit the water below. This was to prevent the raft from buckling in the middle, as had the preceding raft. Then, in a squatting position, we would paddle furiously to prevent the raft from getting stuck in the falling water below. Suddenly we were moving, and we were approaching the top line of the waterfall, sideways as planned. All one could see ahead, or rather sideways, was a horizontal line that was the beginning of the waterfall. Beyond that there was nothing but air. There was, however, a thin cloud of spray rising from the water below. From this vantage point one could also see an occasional foamy crest of water that would appear and disappear above the waterfall line. This was caused from a violent wave or trough that was forced up from the churning river below. Accompanying this rather terrifying vista was a thunderous roar.

Surprisingly, and with great control by Mike, we approached the top horizontal line of the falls, quite slowly and deliberately. We then braced ourselves for the expected ninety-degree freefall, which would be in concert with the cascading water traveling to our mutual destination below. However, at this very moment before the fall, something completely unexpected happened which could never be predicted. I'm not certain if my eyes were closed at this point, but just as Mike yelled, "Hang on", and we all grabbed the side-ropes in anticipation of the drop ... just as we waited for that familiar feeling in your stomach when you're on a carnival ride, and you know it's going to plummet from a great height ... just at that very suspended moment ... nothing happened ... absolutely nothing. There we were, hands welded to the ropes, bodies rigid, faces contorted ... and we were suspended as in space, hung up on a large rock shelf at the drop-point of the falls. It was both absurd and bizarre as we stared in disbelief at the incredible volume of water flowing beneath us, and all around us. Everything was moving, yet we were stuck at the waterfall's edge, motionless.

Everyone who had gone before us, and who were now waiting below, stared in disbelief. The shocked cameraman, who was filming our white water adventure for a post trip souvenir CD, waved at us in surprise from a distance. He wanted to film this unique event. Eventually one of our Aussie teammates nervously peeked over the side of the raft, saw the cameraman waving at us, and very cautiously released one hand to give a tiny, nervous return wave of a few fingers, while Mike started pushing on the rock shelf below with his paddle. Our raft remained determinedly secure. Everything seemed to become suspended, both our raft and time itself. Dangling at the edge of a waterfall in a rubber dinghy, we all had a clear vision of what was probably going to happen, and it wasn't optimistic. The thunderous roar from the falls, the feel of the water below on the raft bottom, and the surrounding clouds of spray all intensified the suspense as we waited ... and waited. Suddenly the raft released.

What occurred next defied all expectations and anticipation, and in fact became hilariously anti-climactic. To everyone's amazement, particularly our own, the survivors below from the previous rafts watched us seemingly in slow motion turn backwards, as our raft went over the falls, rear first, then re-emerged from the force of the water below to float effortlessly away, and out of trouble. We were all facing backwards, hanging on, and it was not possible to paddle. The way the events unfolded, our whole strategy was now useless. But it seemed as if the raft itself knew a better way, and was pursuing its own course. Without a lot of credit to ourselves, we had nonetheless been allowed to inadvertently conquer this one part of the Nile, this one time. Cheering as if it had all been planned from the beginning, and exhilarated at having avoided a near repeat of our previous traumatic spill on Razorback, we all raised and clapped our paddles in the rafters 'high five'. What the others below didn't know about the execution of our strategy could remain a secret of the Nile.

Rafting Photos With Permission of NRE Video Productions

Roaring Thunder Rapids

Leaving the area of the falls we were now on the last leg of our Nile journey. After traversing yet another quiet body of water, we were told we would have to portage an area that had three grade 6 rapids side by side, and that it would be too dangerous to navigate. One of the rapid channels was called the Dead Dutchman, named after a Boer from South Africa who had attempted to shoot the channel without first inspecting it. It was apparently six days before his body popped to the surface, held down by the force and grip of the water.

At this location, the plan would be to drag our rafts around and over some small cliffs, and re-enter into some water leading to a grade 5 drop, with the 'Ashtray' to greet us if we tipped or didn't navigate the run properly. I pondered the origin of the name 'Ashtray', and pictured a cigarette being butted out … or a raft. Having completed the required maneuvers, the rafts re-entered the water and the first one set off. It was successful. The second raft set off, tipped, but was able to regroup and get its rafters back on board. This time we would be the third raft in the sequence, and we set off. It was like clockwork this time, as the team worked in unison, and we arrived upright … pleased at our run. The paddles clicked in another 'high five'. We returned to the river's edge by a back eddy, and there we waited for the final raft that, when having completed its run, would conclude our 30 kilometre Nile adventure. We got the signal the last raft was on its way, entering the rapids named 'Roaring Thunder'. Immediately we could see it bob and bounce in the white churning water. They were in trouble. Suddenly, eight bodies were tossing and popping all around in violent water, all out of control.

"Pull," yelled Mike, and everyone in our raft sprang into action. Though we were fatigued, we clearly recalled our own misadventure on Razorback, and looked on a similar scene where the rapids had spilled bodies everywhere. The recovery kayaks were already at work, trying to gather the rafters swirling around. The kayaks were attempting to bring the emptied rafters to us, since we were the only raft available. They arrived sputtering, coughing and fatigued, but thankful to be pulled into our raft. With the last rafter finally accounted for, we paddled for shore. This was the last rapid on our trip, and at this point we would leave the water, concluding our white water adventure.

Leaving our rafts to be taken by the attendants up a steep bank, we slowly began the climb. Before crawling into the back of the open truck for our return, I gave one last reminiscent look at the Nile below us. From this height and distance, its calmness seemed in such contrast to the stretches of angry white water into which we had slipped when its mood had changed. But we all knew this ancient river had gifted us an experience of a lifetime, and it would not soon be forgotten. Fatigued, but fully satiated by our adventure, we sat quietly on our wooden benches as the truck bumped down the dusty back roads that wound among local huts and hovels. There would be many stories for the campsite in the evening.

Rafting Photos With Permission of NRE Video Productions

To Eldoret, Kenya
*A Spectacle for Locals; Crossing the Border; Touring a Blanket Factory;
Some Signs of Unrest; The Rift Valley*

Safari Day 4

We were up at 5:00 am to take down our tents. After a safari breakfast, we were heading toward the southeastern border of Uganda and on into Kenya. From here we would ascend into the highlands to the city of Eldoret, and onto a nearby campsite called Riverside.

Leaving the ochre-coloured trails of Bujegali behind, village after village appeared and disappeared as we continued westward. Each of these centres in turn consisted of adjoining brick hovels and huts that crowded together on both sides of the road. Markets seemed to blend into other markets as barely a kilometre went by without seeing locals either selling or buying something. However, between the clusters of these busy commercial areas, were interspersed rural stretches where small, round mud huts with thatched roofs stood surrounded by any combination of cows, goats, stacks of home-made bricks, rows of hoed potato hills, patches of maize, sugar cane or banana plants. Although by western standards, one would judge many of the structures we saw to represent a landscape of poverty, they were still in significant contrast to the more occasional pockets observed where I saw only a few boards or sections of metal leaned together to make the barely recognizable rudiments of a shelter. Yet even here, where semi-naked children played among roaming chickens and smoky fires, there came waves, smiles or shouts of greeting. We were kept busy returning the friendly gestures.

As the landscape began to change in elevation, in the higher areas were seen larger fields of sugar cane. In the lower marshy or swampy areas in this part of the country I was surprised to see an abundance of rice growing in the wet, fertile soil. I realized that Uganda is a very fertile country with an abundance of moisture, and with lots of food grown by its inhabitants. There seemed no evidence of throngs of people starving.

A Spectacle for Locals
Beyond the rice fields, and continuing to ascend in elevation, we began to see plots of gum trees, pines and enormous fig trees. At one point in this setting we pulled over to have our routine lunch. Karoma and Tasha, together with our safari attendants, John and Nicholas, began to set up the tables and folding chairs and set about preparing one of our typical traveling safari mid-day meals: fresh sliced avocado and tomato for our bread; cold cuts and barbecue chicken from last evening's meal; small boiled potatoes; shredded cabbage and carrot salad; and slices of fresh pineapple, watermelon, passion fruit, fingerling bananas and mango. In fact, whatever healthy food was grown in the local area, we could expect that it might be added to the daily menu. With this spread before us, we did not know however, that as we ate we would also become an entertaining spectacle for a growing crowd of local onlookers.

The roads in Africa are lined with a constant traffic of pedestrians and others on old bikes, heading in one direction or another. Perhaps it was therefore not surprising that at first a few, then a few more passersby, began stopping to see what was happening with a passenger truck pulled off the road, and several mzungus milling around. For them it was obviously not a familiar site, and therefore worthy of some investigation. First a nearby family of a few adults and children parked themselves to watch the spectacle unfolding before them. Before long, a crowd had gathered. They all stood a short distance away from where we were sitting ... and eating. Soon this gathering in turn attracted an even larger crowd, and observing us suddenly had become an entertaining social event. They not only openly and unabashedly stared at us having lunch, but they also chatted among themselves, often pointing and gesturing. I can only but imagine what conversations they were having.

In addition to their fascination with us in this milieu, it was also obvious they were somewhat in awe of Karoma, our safari leader. After all, here was an indigenous black Masai with his white wife, confidently and competently not only assisting the crew in the preparation of an elaborate lunch, but also demonstrating admirable social skills, leadership, and interacting with his white foreign clients. Equally as astounding and impressive was that he owned a new, enormously large, green safari truck. They must have deduced he was incredibly successful, worthy of their fascination and respect. Of course none of this phased our nonchalant Karoma in the least, but after seeing this wonderful spectacle, I'm certain our local crowd believed that absolutely anything in Africa might be possible after all. The food was great, but I think we were all a little self conscious about the crowd of persistent stares- especially from the more obvious hungry ones.

A spectacle for locals

Crossing the Border

Nearing the southern border, between Uganda and Kenya, we encountered road crews that were repairing a long stretch of the two-lane highway on which we were traveling. We then bumped along at various speeds which in places slowed to as low as 7 km per hour. Passing through a hilly, almost mountainous region, we eventually arrived at the Ugandan-Kenyan border. It was easy to discern that we were approaching the border some distance away because of what seemed to be acres of trucks, crowded together. Some trucks formed long lines, some were parked helter-skelter on both sides of the road as far as the eye could see, and others were grouped in what might otherwise appear as the truck version of an enormous car lot. However, what we were seeing is apparently very typical as trucks prepare to cross the border. We were told that in order to complete the required weighing, searching, inspecting and processing of trucks, at times it could take up to as much as a week for the border to be crossed. I thought it was no wonder that it is apparently not uncommon for a bit to be paid "under the table" to expedite everything.

Apprehensive about how long it might take us to cross the border in the midst of this metal and rubber city, we were surprised to find ourselves rolling past the endless queue of trucks. When we stopped, Tasha took our passports and entered the immigration office to obtain for us the required entry Visas. In the interval, this gave the usual hockers an opportunity to approach the side of the truck and to try to sell various woodcarvings, beaded bracelets, water, pop or food items. However, John and Nicholas had already descended the stairs and were acting as security on our behalf. In no time Tasha had returned, and we immediately crossed into Kenya only to see on this side of the border another approaching line of truck traffic that stretched for 2 to 3 kilometres. Although the trucks were stopped dead, all the diesel motors were still running and spilling black smoke into the air. You could taste the resulting smog, and although it was all a fascinating scene to have observed, we were happy to be traveling on our way.

It was 7:00 pm by the time we arrived at Riverside Campground. However, we were pleased to discover our campsite was an upscale combination of campground and lodge. The buildings have been uniquely structured reflecting an African architectural theme, with a bar connected by a passageway that somewhat produces the illusion of traveling through a cavern or tunnel. Nearby, a small waterfall was spilling into a lower pool, giving it a rather exotic appearance. That evening, under a large thatched roof building in the campsite, we hungrily enjoyed our evening safari meal. With the long traveling day behind us, and a dark African sky brilliant with stars, it was not long after that we all retired into our tents.

Riverside Lodge and Campsite

Touring a Blanket Factory

A tour had been arranged for us at a blanket factory in Eldoret, one of Kenya's larger cities in the southwest. The manufacturing we had seen so far in the towns and villages through which we had passed, was basically individuals making goods by hand. In contrast, here there were a surprising number of employees using higher-end manufacturing equipment for every part of the process. A variety of wool products, such as wool sweaters and a multitude of other garments, are produced in this factory, and the blankets for which it is renowned are actually made from recycled cuttings and leftover material from these products. Also interesting was that everything made here originates from single threads spun from bulk raw wool, all produced right in the factory. As our guide showed us around, we observed that most everything was done by machine, including the dying and the embroidering. After completion, the finished products are destined solely for markets in Britain.

Seeing the whole process from the spinning of threads to the sewing together of various components to complete the finished garment or other product was very interesting. I thought there must be some acknowledged pride in sending such fashionable products to British markets. However, I noticed on one bundle of ready-to-be exported packaged material the label "Made in Taiwan", and under it in almost indiscernible tiny letters, the additional phrase, "via Mombassa". This surprised me, and I realized it is doubtful Kenya or Kenyans will ever get credit for the manufacturing done by its workers when their products are sold in fashionable stores in Britain.

Although we had a guide on our tour, we felt free to wander and chat with the busy workers. A female employee seated at a sewing machine, attaching sleeves to the body of a garment, was asked by one of our group how much she was paid for her work. She replied she was paid in shillings for the piecework quantity she completed, which usually amounted to about 150 sweaters. A quick calculation gave her an equivalent daily wage of about $8.

Some Signs of Unrest

Leaving Eldoret, we launched into a countryside that varied from large maize fields to even larger tracts planted in wheat. After traveling for about a half hour from Eldoret, we noticed that a few occasional buildings had been burned or destroyed. The other buildings on each side remained untouched. Some distance further we noticed the same thing, then again a few kilometres along. We were then told these were either Kikuyu businesses or residences. In this part of Kenya, Kikuyus are in the minority to the general population of Masai. Although not nearly as prominent as we had been led to believe in the media, this however was some evidence of the violence that had broken out in Kenya about two months earlier. It seemed so out of character from what we had seen of the people to date.

The more obvious signs of the unrest, however, were the two tent villages we saw on the outskirts on both sides of Eldoret. These could be seen while traveling along the main road. Again we were informed that these were Kikuyus who had been forced out of their homes, and who were remaining in the white canvas tent villages until they could be relocated. However, this was the only time in Kenya that we were exposed to these signs of unrest.

Some signs of unrest

The Rift Valley
After traveling some distance from Eldoret, our safari truck continued to gain altitude. With the canopy sides open I began to layer up because of the slight chill. Eventually we approached an incredible viewpoint. Here we made a brief stop to absorb the view that unfolded before us- a huge valley below, so vast that the distant high hills on the opposite side appeared only as a misty blue ridge. We had arrived at the famous Rift Valley. The valley is caused by an actual rift in the earth's crust, which stretches approximately 6,000 miles from the Mediterranean in the north to Mozambique in the southeast. In East Africa, it runs for about 5,000 kilometres, and here the valley can vary in width from 30 to 100 kilometres.

After standing and scanning the vista for some time, and taking numerous photographs, we began the switchback descent. As we snaked down, the vegetation at this location was a luscious green with many varieties of trees, including some in full dress of brilliant maroon blossoms. Other trees were covered in deep orange flowers. One could not help but stare while soaking up the passing beauty.

At the bottom of the valley we found a more semi-arid region, with innumerable goats of all colours that were grazing among the acacia trees and brush. You could easily tell that the villages in this region were far less affluent than those seen closer to the top. After traveling along the lower valley bottom for some time, we again ascended its south side where the increased rainfall once again made the landscape green. But it wasn't long before we were again heading down and into what now became an extremely dry environment, as seen by its geography and type of vegetation: cactus trees; thorny bushes; smaller flat-top acacia trees; a rocky and dusty ground surface; a hot temperature. The heat became that of an oven. Here the progress of *JuJu*, our safari truck, was extremely slow as we crawled over sections of road that had been washed out by flash floods, and were now only dry riverbed skeletons. After some time traveling in the heat, combined with the tossing and swaying of the truck as we traversed one dry riverbed after another, the long journey was having its first tell-tale signs on its safari passengers.

All of a sudden, with perfect timing, viewed ahead was a huge lake ... brown in colour. We had arrived at Lake Baringo, our camp destination.

Overlooking the Rift Valley

Traveling the valley floor

At Lake Baringo
Crocodile Smiles; Fish Eagles and Hippos; To a Pokot Village

Safari Days 5-6

Crocodile Smiles

Lake Baringo is classed as a fresh water lake even though it does have a slight sodium content. It can however support tilapia and catfish, and has an enormous variety of birds including the large regal Fish Eagle. The colour of the lake is actually brown due to all the salty sediment that erodes into it. When our truck pulled into the campsite, Karoma gave us two cautions before we began to set up our tents. First, we were to be careful at the water's edge because of the crocodiles that would be sunning themselves, or swimming near the shore. Second, we were to use our halogen headlamps or flashlights to check carefully around us at night before walking to the toilets. This was because hippos often leave the water at night to graze on the vegetation that is also found around the campsite. If there had been any doubt before, we now definitely knew we were on an African safari.

As the tents were being set up not far from the water's edge, someone announced that a short distance away the first crocodile had been spotted. Although it was only about six feet in length, it was bathing in the sun with its mouth open and exposing some serious looking teeth. For a moment I wondered if this open-mouthed, sharp-toothed crocodile smile was a result of it watching us set up camp ... so very conveniently nearby. It occurred to me that a bunch of safari flesh, camping right on a crocodile's doorstep, might be for it the closest thing to 'take out'.

Later in the early evening, just after the sun set, someone announced that a hippo had been seen grazing on bushes directly behind the toilets. However, we were also told that a local camp attendant would be keeping watch during the night, and would chase away the hippos ... with a stick. There was understandably some apprehension when our group crawled into their respective tents that evening. I saw the stick ... it was not long!

Fish Eagles and Hippos

After a 7:30 breakfast, our safari troop trekked a short distance down a trail to two open-hull boats, and set off to cruise some of the nearby shoreline of Lake Baringo. Two crocodiles were seen sun bathing out of the water, and we spotted a couple of four-foot monitor lizards. Two local fishermen were also in the area. They were each seated on a balsam structure that was a collection of balsam poles latched together in a half-boat shape. It was pointed at the bow but had no stern whatever. There was no depth to these flotation boats, and the individual fisherman sat directly on the bottom and propelled it by using their hands or hand paddles. The fishermen waved, and were eager to hold up tilapia that had been caught with a single line thrown into the water.

Our destination was then to head to a nearby island that was known as the fishing territory of several Fish Eagles. Even from a distance, we could recognize the shape of a large Fish Eagle perched high in a tree. As we approached, our boat guides began to whistle in imitation of its call. Having attracted its attention, a small fish was then thrown in the water. Within seconds the eagle took flight, and with huge wings spread it glided to where the fish had been thrown. At the last moment, with claws thrust forward and talons open, the fish was neatly plucked from the water as the eagle flapped away to a high branch. It was an awesome display that proved the white hooded, regal eagle is worthy of its name.

Our boats then sped to the far shore, about fifteen minutes away. En route, a crocodile was spotted swimming in open water, but soon we arrived among trees and bushes that were poking through the water's surface, which before flooding had been dry land. The area had a marshy appearance and we slowly cruised in and out of the larger channels, looking for hippos that were expected to be found in this region.

Soon someone pointed to several female hippos and their calves, most of them partly submerged and crowded in a close group. This collection was viewed from a cautious distance, particularly with the presence of the calves, and no one on board was prepared to dispute this strategy. Having feasted for a while on this African vista of rising and sinking hippos, occurring amid their vocalizations of grunts and snorts, we then went looking for any solitary bulls that might be found nearby. It did not take long to spot two partially submerged bulls that were routinely flicking their tiny ears that seemed so out of place on their massive, bulky heads. We were reminded how quickly these often cantankerous creatures could effortlessly overturn a boat by surfacing underneath, and we kept our distance. By the time we began to boat back to our camp, we were totally satisfied with the day's wildlife excursion, including seeing several ostriches grazing among the mixture of cattle and goats near the shore. One could not but conclude that it had been a wonderful African safari morning, fulfilling all expectations.

To A Pokot Village
We ate our lunch under our canopy with a few opened-mouthed, sunbathing crocs looking on. Perhaps it was my imagination that I thought they seemed to be looking our way, and wondered if they might be thinking of lunch too. We had a few short hours to relax before our next activity, just enough time for a quick nap. I also had time to stretch out in the African sunshine and read some of Nelson Mandela's book, *Walk To Freedom*, that I had brought with me. We then boarded *JuJu* to have what for me would be one of the most significant experiences of a lifetime, a visit to a remote traditional village of the nomadic Pokot people.

We followed a defined road for some time. I was astonished when we not only left the road to travel a dusty trail, but then even left the trail onto a hard-packed, desert-like surface to weave in and out of cacti, dry scrub brush and short, flat-topped acacias. There were no signs that suggested people might live here, but the local guide that Karoma had brought with us was still able to lead us to the perimeter of a very primitive village. At one moment we were seemingly wandering aimlessly in the bush of Africa, the next moment we were looking at a small crowd of Pokots. As we descended the truck, we were in the middle of slender young men, women of various ages, and a few children. Behind this group, like a half dozen candles in a circle on a cake, small cone-shaped huts were arranged at a short distance from each other. In the middle was a barrier of thorny acacia brush that keep livestock in at night. The adults wore their daily colourful traditional dress, and the youngest children ran around without clothes, or only tops. The young men had thin bright red or blue blankets hung over one shoulder, draping also over their equally bright loincloth-style waist skirts. They could use these blankets as protection from the elements or as cover on a chilly night. The women were heavily jeweled with hoops and bracelets, and wore large plate-like, multi-coloured beaded collars that waved up and down when they moved.

Karoma was detailed in the information he gave us on the surviving lifestyle of this group of nomads. Since it was the dry season, the men had taken their cattle about 30 kilometres to where they had access to water. However, a small group of young men, and the woman and children, all remained in the village. It was this group that greeted us in their own language and shook each of our hands on our arrival. For all the reputation we had heard of the aggressiveness of these people, they were very hospitable and accommodating in letting us take pictures and allowing us to enter their very simple, small mud huts. The young men were pleased to give us displays of bow and arrow shooting, nor did it take much encouragement for them to begin clapping, singing and jump-dancing to the rhythm of shaking bells, which some wore. They even insisted some of our group join them. I was aware that this was another rare and fascinating African moment, as my camera clicked continuously. We had been transported not only into an entirely different world, but seemingly into an equally different period of time. There was almost a sense of unreality as I gazed on these people who, in contrast with us, seemed so comfortably situated and integrated into this strangely beautiful, but harsh environment. It was difficult to understand how they could survive here, yet they seemed to have everything they needed, including that most rare of all commodities… contentment. This was especially evident inside their tiny, windowless huts.

The cramped, small space of their huts seemed to provide for them all the necessities: sapling bed; sapling bench; campfire; supporting pole on which to hang things including the bow and arrow; space under the bed for the baby goat; a couple of cooking containers. There were also hollow gourds filled with various plants and herbs known only to them, and taken from the dry, semi-arid land. A special horn hung from the centre support pole away from the reach of children, and contained many traditional medicines and remedies. In some ways it was like the household medicine cabinet or first aid kit. Although you had to stoop low to enter the half-size doorway, this miniature shelter gave the impression it contained everything essential. And outside the hut, where the Pokots were now dancing for us, it was hard to imagine that when traveling into the Pokot region it is apparently recommended it be with an armed guard only. It made us appreciate the special advantage we had in going on safari with Karoma.

As we were driving back to our campsite on Lake Baringo, we passed through a village. Because of their unique dress, we easily identified some Pokot women who had made the journey to the village on foot. Karoma told us that they occasionally walk to the nearby village market to supplement their diet of mixed milk and blood with some maize or tilapia fish. They might sell or trade a goat for currency. We were also told that since the cattle had been herded 30 kilometres into the interior, young boys were sent back home regularly to bring fresh cows' milk, particularly for the young children. Such stories only spoke further of the resiliency of these people. The question came to mind: how long in this rapidly shrinking world could this ancient life-style be preserved?

Last Night at Lake Baringo Camp- The Night Hippo

When we returned to our campsite, it was time to sit back in a folding camp chair, sip on a Kenyan Tusker beer, and watch the lingering light cast shadows on Lake Baringo. For our last night, the lake gifted us with one of its wonderful African sunsets.

Later that night, when we were all in our tents sleeping, I was awakened by the bark of a dog. Looking through the netted windows of my tent, I could barely make out a larger moving shadow nearby, then another. There was some accompanying shuffling noise, followed by thuds that I discerned came from something bumping or brushing against the support ropes from another tent. The shadows moved past and beyond my tent at a very slow pace, and obviously without fear and in no hurry. Detecting no more disturbance or movement, I fell back to sleep.

In the morning I made a point of speaking to the Kenyan camp attendant who had been guarding our campsite at night. He confirmed two hippos had come ashore in the night and wandered through our campsite. I asked him if there were ever any incidents with the hippos, and he told me they are the single most dangerous animals in all Africa. This is because the greatest number of people are killed by them, even more than deaths by crocodiles. I had to ask him if he had ever been charged by a hippo in the course of trying to drive them out of the campsite. He told me he had, but that he escaped by deliberately running in a zigzag pattern through the trees. He said that if you run in a straight line, a hippo would easily overtake you. He then informed me that a month ago one of the fisherman casting his net from his small balsam boat was attacked and killed by a rogue hippo bull.

I left Lake Baringo with many rich memories of our time there, and with a much-increased respect for the hippopotamus.

To Nakuru
Lake Nakuru Game Reserve; Animal Searching;
Busy Baboons, Copulating Cats and Gangly Giraffes; The Black Rhino

Safari Days 7-8

Lake Nakuru Game Reserve
In the morning we left Lake Baringo, and the terrain became gradually greener as we progressed toward the small city of Nakuru. At one point on this journey we stopped at a curio market that had a few souvenir kiosks, including several hand-crafted items. This was the place where one crosses the equator, and there was a large sign that displayed this significance. Closer to Nakuru I was surprised to see not only larger tracks of maize, but large flowing fields of green wheat. On the road, we even passed a small harvester, the only one I saw in East Africa. Although Nakuru is a small city, the town square boasts three banks, a tourist market filled with woodcarvings, masks, and 'tie and dye' wall hangings of various sizes. Just down from the market was a place I could finally send off an e-mail. We did not stay long in town however, and within an hour we were off to what we had really come to see ... the Lake Nakuru Game Reserve

We made a short stop to register at the entry gate, and continued on to the campsite. It was situated on the edge of the reserve, but with no fences or barriers it is also open to wandering game animals. When we arrived, the camp was already overrun with monkeys, and as quickly as we set up our tents they were sitting arrogantly on top of them. A small baby monkey enjoyed playfully swinging back and forth on one of the tent ropes that angled to a peg in the ground. Those monkeys not sitting on tents were running around the campsite, or climbing up and down the large trees.

Tents up, we immediately boarded *JuJu* to get in a few hours of safari game-searching around the perimeter of a lake situated in the middle of the game reserve. As we drove toward the lake, what greeted us was absolutely amazing. There were zebras everywhere. Large African buffalos with heavy bow-shaped horns were scattered across the plain. On the lake itself, huge pelicans swam back and forth in unison. Flamingos formed a pink line in the distance, further out. Looking around, there were crowds of gazelles, impalas, and waterbuck. In fact, the game was so prolific it was difficult to grasp it all.

And the rhinos! That afternoon alone we calculated we saw over 50 white rhinos ... standing... laying... drinking... sparring with their horns ... staring passively or aggressively ... young with their mothers ... old ostracized bulls ... and all wild, and all free. The camera went into overtime with these magnificent creatures.

As the light dimmed, we began our return to camp. It was then I noticed one rhino a short distance away from the safari truck, intently looking at us ... head held high. Tossing his head, he started walking toward us. The vehicle continued traveling very slowly. His ears were pointed forward, and he sustained his aggressive focus on the moving truck. Suddenly he broke into a trot, then a gallop, heading straight toward us. By then we had increased our speed and were out of his range, and I saw it pull up. But I remained impressed with this rhino gesture, and with both the wonder and excitement at having seen the display of aggressiveness. It reinforced the understanding that Lake Nakuru Reserve can be a dangerous place for one to be alone, and out of a vehicle.

White Rhino

We were in our tents early that night, for we knew that we had to be off by 5:30 am. at the latest if we were to spot any of the nocturnal animals still lingering about, or if we were to see any of the early risers. It was still dark when we set off looking for the elusive leopard, the lion, and with the hope of seeing the very rare black rhino. I was surprised to find out how cold it could be at this altitude on the flats of the Nakuru plain, and began to layer up against the chill. I had to keep my hands in my pockets to help warm them. For the first part of this early morning we kept to the bush trails where we discovered a decaying carcass, no doubt left over from a kill. We continued to see much of the game we had seen the afternoon before, but one could not stop looking and marveling at what by now was becoming the familiar. After all, viewing was the essence of a safari .... to be inhaled, savoured and enjoyed. No matter how many times I saw the same types of animals, I could not tire of looking at them.

Busy Baboons, Copulating Cats and Gangly Giraffes

Eventually the bush in which we traveled lessened, and we came upon a tribe of baboons. They seemed totally unconcerned by our approach, as they went about their baboon business of collecting food, sitting on their haunches while eating, scurrying, scrapping and engaging in the more intimate act of grooming. As I was taking a photo of one dominant male grooming a smaller female, he suddenly rotated to her back, mounted her and carried out a quick, but intense, copulation ... to the astonishment of the inadvertent voyeurs on the safari truck. With surprised safari-mouths still open, he dismounted and returned in front of her to continue his casual grooming, as if nothing had happened. We were definitely experiencing Africa at its most natural. "Just like a male", came a remark from one of the female safari passengers, to a response of laughter.

As *JuJu* continued rocking along the game reserve's dusty roads, Karoma announced that he had spotted a pride of three lions. Earlier in the morning we had seen a huge paw print the size of both my hands, so we knew they were in the area. There was excitement. Again Karoma slowly drove to the sighting where a dominant male was with a female. A slightly smaller brother of the male was a respectful distance away from the pair, and two African buffalo bulls were intently focused on the younger brother. The staring bulls looked as if they were prepared to charge the second male lion, if necessary. My camera was ready, and I began clicking to capture this classic African scene.

As if being filmed for a National Geographic documentary, we watched in awe at what then unfolded before us. The female was in heat, and we were treated to the courting ritual of these majestic cats. With the dominant male laying beside his mate, the female then playfully rolled onto her back, with paws in the air. This obviously excited the male, for when she rolled back into a crouching position, she was instantly mounted by the male whose copulation was as quick as had been that of the male baboon we had seen mating earlier. Constantly moving at short distances, the two lions repeated this breeding tradition while the younger brother continued to follow, but also at his same respectful distance.

Continuing this process, the male and female drew closer to the safari truck, unconcerned that it was now almost in their path. Then, with little attention to us, the female passed within a few feet, and to the other side of our vehicle. The male followed, allowing us to capture unbelievable close-ups. The second male eventually followed its older brother and his mate, and also made his way around the truck. The whole experience seemed palpable, so much so that it reinforced what Karoma and Tasha had named their safari, 'The Touch of Africa'. And again, Africa had also touched me.

Eventually we continued along the flat, open plain scattered with acacia trees. It was here that something the same height as the trees caught my eye. As the truck inched closer, I started to distinguish the heads of giraffes from the acacia branches. Closer still, these heads became attached to long necks, which became attached to bodies supported on four spindly legs. It was amazing to see how the giraffe's tongue could carefully pluck the acacia leaves from among a dense thicket of sharp thorns, each up to three or more inches long. One of these thorns had actually punctured my sandal while in a campsite. We came so close to these incredible creatures that I felt as if I could reach out and touch them. Later, when we rounded a small hill, we surprised another group of giraffes made up of a few females with several young of various ages and sizes. Although they sped away quickly, their ambling, slow motion gait was exaggerated even more by the waving movement of their necks, like the action of a pendulum.

The Black Rhino
As if the morning had not already given us the most amazing close encounters with wildlife, we were in for another special treat ... viewing the African black rhino. "You are extremely lucky this morning," Karoma said softly over the PA system. He continued, "Over there, with the two other rhinos, is the rare black rhino."

We were told that because of its devastation from hunting and poaching, there are apparently only about 2500 black rhinos remaining in the world. Karoma explained to us that the black rhino was easily distinguished from the white rhino because, as a bush browser, the black rhino held its head high. On the other hand, as grazers, the white rhinos had evolved a massive head close to ground level. The back rhino also had a much smaller pointed mouth, more suitable for feeding in the bushes, whereas the whites had wide flat mouths, again adapted to grazing.

Realizing how fortunate we were to see one of the few surviving black rhinos, brought nearly to extinction by our own guilty species, we sat in both silence and reverence as we soaked in the significance. It was at this point that I quietly resolved to share this powerful experience with others, and in so doing, to encourage them to go on their own safari to be able to feel the deep impact of such a 'stolen moment'.

When we arrived back at camp for lunch, scattering a few monkeys that had decided to move in during our absence, the excitement of the morning animal search persisted. Multiple conversations that shared what for each of us were individual highlights, continued to erupt. Knowing I was keeping copious notes on all our experiences, one in the group asked facetiously what I might call this chapter in my travel diary. I thought for a moment, then suggested that with all the mating in the wild we had witnessed this day, I had the option of choosing between the titles of "The Fornicating Safari" or "Banging Baboons and Copulating Cats". I compromised on 'Busy Baboons'.

The black rhino in the forefront

To Lake Naivasha
Wandering Hippo; Trekking Naivasha Wildlife Park; Ngondi Village School;
Mama Wainaina's Meal; Elsamere- the 'Born Free' Connection

Safari Days 9-10

Leaving Nakuru we were now heading east toward Lake Naivasha. The highway was generally much improved as we sailed past larger agricultural tracts of land. Eventually we turned off the main road and continued to travel until we came to the lake, then began to circumnavigate part of it. We were surprised to encounter greenhouse after greenhouse where roses and other flowers are grown for the European market. The flowers are taken to the Nairobi airport where they are quickly exported to cities such as London or Amsterdam.

Although impressive commerce for Kenya, Karoma informed us that this industry has also presented some challenges to the area in that over the years huge water reserves have been sucked out of the lake to support the greenhouses. The resulting drop in water level of the lake has been so significant that one area called Crescent Island has now become part of the mainland. A second challenge resulting from the industry has been related to the dense housing accommodations built to support the workers. They have created an environment where social problems have become significant: rampant A.I.D.S.; prostitution; and crime. As we passed the gateway to one of the series of housing buildings, I read a huge sign posted at the gate entrance, "Do You Know Most Laborers Don't Know Their HIV Status".

Wandering Hippo
Our large campsite at Lake Naivasha had huge acacia trees. Around the campsite was an electric fence consisting of two lines of thick wire attached to short posts. Caution signs explained that the fence was electrified at night to keep grazing hippos away from the tent area. In the evening, while we were sitting around the campsite, it didn't take long before someone announced that the shadowy outline of a hippo had been spotted. It was wandering near the fence, grazing on short grass that bordered large papyrus reeds growing in the shallows of Lake Naivasha. Grabbing our miniature halogen headlamps, we slowly advanced in the darkness to investigate this wandering hippo.

Even though we had been cautioned about the erratic and aggressive behaviour of hippos in general, the charged electric fence gave us some confidence, and we were able to get very close. The dark brown shading of the hippo's back looked almost black in the night, but in the light of our headlamps I was amazed to see how bright pink the entire underside was. When partially submerged in the water during the day, one is not usually able to notice this contrast of colouring as much. It was also surprising to see how our hippo effortlessly balanced its enormous weight on such tiny hippo hoofs, while on land. The grazing hippo did not seem the least interested in our presence, and continued to wander along the fence line munching away to fill its large belly before retreating back into the lake to protect itself from the next day's sun. As I retired to my tent, I took some solace that this hippo would not be bumping into my tent ropes, as had the other hippos at Lake Baringo. I also thought about how perplexing it was to have just seen this peaceful animal grazing, that at other times is regarded as one of the most feared killers in Africa.

Trekking Lake Naivasha Wildlife Park (Crescent Island)
In the morning we were transported to a private animal park on the other side of Lake Naivasha. This park was unique in that we would be able to trek relatively safely on foot through the park, since there were no rhinos or African buffalo to charge us. However, the park was teeming with many other African animals and the scenery was so classic that it was also where some of the movie "Out of Africa" had been filmed. We would actually be trekking on Crescent Island, which in fact is no longer an island, but now a part of the mainland because of all the water that over the years has been pumped from the lake to support the greenhouse industry. Yet, here the animals can roam freely. The area is also a small part of a vast animal corridor that extends a great distance beyond, and up into the

mountainous regions above. From the very beginning I found myself experiencing a wonderful day's adventure. Contrasted with much of our animal viewing to date (which was done from the vantage point of the safari truck), here we were on foot and gazing upon nearby herds, or looking up at a multitude of wild giraffes. With my head stretched back, I watched them casually plucking acacia leaves from the trees. From the ground, and at close quarters, it gave an entirely different perspective. Gazing around in a circle, I stared at the herds of antelopes, waterbucks, gazelles, gnus and wildebeests. These were all viewed with Lake Naivasha, and the numerous surrounding mountains, serving as the framed backdrop. The whole scenario for me seemed to represent Africa, in a microcosm.

After having trekked for some time, we returned to where the safari truck had been parked under a grove of acacias, providing some much appreciated shade. Here our camp attendants, John and Nicholas, had prepared for us a special lunch that included champagne and orange juice, served in our 'Out of Africa' setting. After lunch we again trekked down to the lake where two boats returned us to our campsite on the other side of the lake. The trip back was a suitable ending to this unique sojourn, especially because we encountered two separate herds of hippos en route. In the heat of the day, most of their bodies were submerged, but their enormous eyes followed us intently as they vigorously twitched their tiny ears. I was amazed to notice that two fishermen were standing waist deep in water, not that far from where the hippos were bathing. The men were working together, casting a net into the deeper water, and then encircling the fish. I recalled the story from Lake Baringo about the fisherman, who on his balsam float, had been charged and killed by a rogue hippo. I began to realize the danger these fishermen faced daily. The fishermen, themselves, were dwarfed by a seemingly impenetrable wall of rising papyrus reeds that grew nearby, and all along the water's edge, towering over them. Finding a break in the papyrus, our boats entered the small bay that led to our campsite. It had been another good African safari day.

Ngondi Village School

Two mini vans were waiting for us in the morning to take us on an off-road journey to the village of Karoma's mother. Here we would tour the local school, adopted by 'The African Touch' as a support project. We would return to the home of Karoma's mother for an indigenous home-cooked meal. The 'Touch of Africa' would become the taste of Africa. The access road from Lake Naivasha to Ngondi village was one of the most challenging I have ever ridden, and for the most part the dirt road followed a dry riverbed that in the rainy season would be flooded with fast moving water. I could imagine what mud there would be. Although the trip was probably only about 8 kilometres, it took us nearly an hour to reach the village. We bumped and clunked along in a permanent cloud of dust, the brown powder often over a foot deep in some areas. Fortunately, oncoming traffic was minimal, for when we did meet another vehicle the dust engulfed us completely for a few minutes before it began to subside. Several members of the group had attached bandanas around their mouths to try to filter out some of the dust, but I found it all added to the adventure and mystique of the experience.

When we arrived at the school, classes were in session but we were greeted enthusiastically just the same, and given a tour. The school buildings were set out in a square configuration, with a bit of a playground or courtyard in the middle. Two of the buildings were of slab wood construction, and at right angles to each other. The intermediate or senior classes were in a stone building at one side of the square. Each building housed about four classrooms. The primary building had cardboard finishing on the interior partitions. Here, shutter-style windows let in minimal light, which allowed me to see a few wall charts that were displayed. Fifty-seven primary students were crammed into the small space that we were told had held over eighty students the preceding year. The sturdier stone intermediate building was newer, with rope-tied rafters and a corrugated metal roof. An additional unfinished building of stone was still under construction, but it already accommodated an administration office currently in use. Donated building materials to finish it were piled outside. We were told that the primary students attended classes from 6:30 am to 4:00 pm, whereas the more senior classes went until 5:30 pm.- a long day by even adult standards.

After visiting a number of classrooms and hearing some wonderful songs, our safari group presented a few modest gifts to student representatives of the school. Two of the gifts were frisbees, which seemed to puzzle the students. Some of the men in our group began demonstrating how they were to be thrown and caught, and soon the students joined them, delighting in the game. From our observations, it was obvious the men were having just as much fun.

Mama Wainaima's Meal

From the school, we enjoyed a one and a half kilometre walk through the village to Mama Wainaima's place. Her house, by village standards, would be considered modern. The exterior was made of slab wood, with western-style pitched-roofs over the main living room and the two adjoining bedrooms. Unique to the house was the small solar panel on the roof that intermittently ran her one-channel television set, and provided some lighting. Mama was waiting for us and gave us all an enthusiastic and warm welcome. She herself is a most vivacious, friendly and hospitable lady, and we all took an immediate liking to her.

As we chatted, and made ourselves comfortable either in her living room or outside in the shade in the dirt-swept courtyard, three other women were preparing the meal in a separate, nearby cookhouse. Peering into the darkness, I saw several steaming pots on a glowing charcoal fire, over which bubbled and sizzled our meal. The aroma was wonderful, but it was over 30 degrees in the small-boarded building, yet the women were dressed in their usual attire that consisted of considerable material. In contrast, I was perspiring in my shorts and light short-sleeved shirt. Soon we were all crowded into Mama's living room where we were treated to substantial and flavourful portions of goat stew, beef and goat cooked meat, and a shredded, cooked cabbage dish loaded with tiny peas .We felt very privileged to have been Mama's guests, and to have been treated to such sumptuous local dishes.

Karoma's mother (Mama Wainaima)

Elsamere- the 'Born Free Connection

After a detour to view some more hippos, and a large congregation of flying and floating flamingoes on one of the shores of Lake Naivasha, we arrived at the beautiful acreage of George and Joy Adamson. They had been the couple that had raised the famous lion Elsa and later released her back into the wild, as described in the novel and movie, 'Born Free'. Elsamere is a beautiful home in a large garden setting that remains intact and overlooks Lake Naivasha from a scenic vantage point. The complex now functions as both a tourist destination and a foundation facility operated in Joy Adamson's name.

Joy Adamson eventually became a conservationist of international renown, particularly after publishing *Born Free* and its sequels. Previous to her own suspected murder, a poacher had murdered her husband, George, who was a game warden. Although a sad and tragic demise for these two, who had such a passion for Africa and its wildlife, the beautiful residence situated atop Lake Naivasha continues Joy Adamson's work. Sitting on the front lawn, and enjoying a traditional 'high tea' with Tasha, Karoma and our group, I had the satisfaction of knowing that the profits from our visit were directed to such a worthy cause.

Onto The Masai Mara
*Entering the Game Reserve; First Elephants; The Phantom Hyena;
Visit to A Masai Village; Balloons and Champagne;
More Magic on the Masai Mara (Photos)*

Safari Days 11-13

Up at 5:30, we broke camp early to eventually take the highway to the town of Narok. We would be approaching Masai country and heading for the Masai Mara, the 15,000 square kilometres of wildlife reserve run by the Masai themselves. As we left Lake Naivasha, at first we viewed larger tracks of maize and wheat. However, this changed into an arid region scattered with flattop acacias and inhabited only by goats and herders. Eventually this more barren region transitioned into larger open areas where, dotted on the open landscape, could now be seen small brilliant patches of bright red. At first I wasn't certain what these almost luminous orange-red spots were. From time to time they appeared to be moving with the herds of cattle that wandered about in the dry, vast plain. It turned out these colourful bright patches, so easily seen from a distance, were actually the blankets and tunics worn by cattle-herding Masai.

At Narok we also saw a number of Masai dressed in their traditional attire of brilliant blankets, beads and jewelry. Continuing onto the Masai Mara we passed several traditional Masai villages. There was no doubt we were in the heart of Masai country. The villages consisted of several square dung-plastered huts all arranged in a circle, and completely enclosed by a larger outer perimeter of thorny acacia brush. This outer protective thicket would be impenetrable to the hyenas or lions that otherwise would attack the cattle.

Entering the Game Reserve
Our safari truck finally arrived at the Masai Mara Game Reserve gate. Here a crowd of colourfully dressed Masai women awaited any visitors to whom they might sell traditional Masai blankets, jewelry and various other curios and souvenirs. Even as I descended the metal fold-down stairs from *JuJu*, I could tell these vendors would be persistent. Aggressive entrepreneurs immediately swarmed me. All the women were talking at once and pushing curios into my hands. Finally I pointed to one of the bright Masai blankets that had so keenly caught my eye when we were traveling out on the plains.

"How much?" I asked in English..
"10,000 shillings," came a reply.
"Too much, too much," I protested.
"How much you pay?" strategically queried another entrepreneur.
"300 shillings," I offered to someone, a bit dubiously.
"No, 700 shillings," someone else countered.
"Too much ... 350 shillings," I counter-countered, not quite certain to whom, but getting caught up in the game.
"OK, 500 shillings ... you have," a Masai compromised.
"No...too much. 400 shillings," I counter-compromised.
"OK...OK... 500 shillings."
"No... 400 shillings... no more."
"OK, OK, OK... 500 shillings."

I wasn't certain if that last bit of bargaining was a language problem or a strategy designed to confuse me, but in the end I managed to barter for a blanket, with a bead necklace thrown in for 500 Kenyan shillings, and everybody left smiling. Everyone that is except the two women who had kept putting their own blankets in turn into my hands, then removing the other woman's blanket at the same time. As I re-boarded our truck, the two women were still arguing furiously about whose blanket I had bought. I actually didn't know myself, but possessively clutched my hard bargained for souvenirs, as we drove through the entry gate and off into the reserve.

The Masai Mara is a northern continuation of the Serengeti, and is primarily a flat plain with some gently rolling areas at the perimeter. It is bordered in the far distance by once volcanic mountains and larger hills, and on our arrival it was covered in dry brown grass. The Masai Mara would be our home for the next three days, and the excitement grew as we anticipated seeing Africa's so called 'Big Five': the elephant; rhino; hippo; lion; and giraffe. Although of the five, the only one we had not yet seen was the elephant, we were still eager to enjoy repeats. One could never tire of viewing exotic African wildlife in a natural environment, and at such close quarters.

First Elephants
It was only a couple of kilometres inside the park when we heard Karoma announce that elephants were ahead. And there they were ...not in a movie ... not on a National Geographic documentary... but looming directly in front of us ... our first elephants of the safari! It was a herd consisting of a huge, dominant matriarch, with some younger females and their various-sized calves. They were grazing, ripping the taller brown grass from the ground with their trunks and casually stuffing it in their mouths, while their ears fanned the air. The calves were very entertaining to watch- sucking from their mothers, playing with other young ones as they trotted around, or staring intently at our safari truck with uncomprehending looks. Finally the heard began to amble away, and we drove on. Moving slowly along the defined dusty trails that are the compulsory routes for all visiting vehicles, we next encountered a number of Masai giraffes. We noticed that the colouring on their patches was much darker than the tawny colour of the giraffes we had seen at Lake Nakuru Park, and were told they were a different species. And so it went as we continued to grind across the Masai Mara toward our campsite, encountering a wide variety of animals: zebras; crown cranes; ostriches; Thompson and Grant gazelles, wart hogs, jackals, hyenas, lines of wildebeests and more elephants. By the time we arrived at our campsite we had already feasted our eyes on many of the African animals we had come to see, and were hungry for viewing more over the next couple of days.

The Phantom Hyena

Our Masai Mara campsite was in an excellent location on a bend in the Mara River. In addition to the tenting area, the campsite also had a main thatched-roofed building which was a combination open air bar, dining room and recreation area. There were also rooms for accommodation. When we arrived, a noisy tribe of baboons was occupying a bend across the small river and were either noisily drinking, screaming at one another, or chasing each other around. It was great to watch them from the lookout platform as they carried on their antics, paying no attention to us. Back at the campsite three Masai warriors wearing their colourful, brilliant red-orange tunics and the traditional Masai blanket, joined us. One carried a Masai spear, which we found out had been handed down from grandfather to father to son. It turned out these Masai were to be our camp security during the night, to ward off any unwelcome animals that might wander into the campsite. Later in the evening, knowing our safety was in good hands, the final tent zipper was closed under a starry African sky.

Shortly after midnight I awoke to noisy baboons. As I peeked out of my tent flap to check on this disturbance, I looked upon what has become a most memorable image for me. In the flickering firelight I saw the frames of the three Masai warriors silhouetted against the orange glow of the fire. Two were seated, and the third Masai was standing near the fire, leaning on his spear. The campfire light was intermittently dancing off him, illuminating his tunic that matched the same brilliant colours as the fire. Smiling at having been inadvertently treated to such a rare but classic African scene, I slipped contentedly back into sleep ... that is until I heard the commotion.

About 3:00 am the serenity of our campsite was shattered by a young woman's scream. This was followed by a thudding noise of sorts that went by my tent, then by a slapping sound. Looking out of my tent door-flap, all I could see at first was darkness, and then the bobbing light from a halogen lamp strapped to someone's head. Two of the Masai were still at the campsite and seemed quite relaxed, so I returned to my sleeping bag to wait until morning to find out what the ruckus had been about.

That morning the exciting gossip was that a hyena had crept into the camp and terrified a girl from another nearby safari group. A Masai had apparently gone to investigate what the scream was all about, and encountered the shadowy form of a hyena lurking in the darkness within the camp. Since the Masai are very reluctant to kill any wild animal, he had instead pursued it and chased it off. No one else had seen the hyena clearly, or they had just caught a glimpse of its shadowy form. It was dubbed the phantom hyena.

It made for a wonderful safari story and I delighted in the content. However, eventually the incident was clarified and the real version of the episode emerged. A girl from the nearby safari group had indeed screamed in the night, but apparently it was because she was having a bad dream. When our camp Masai had gone to find out what was going on, he did discover that a hyena had wandered into the campsite near where the girl had been sleeping. He ran after it, chasing it out of the camp. The thudding noise I had heard was the sound of the hyena running past my tent, and the flapping noise was the Masai warrior chasing after it in his sandals. Although not quite the dramatic African safari scenario of the original version, in the end I was satisfied there was still some mystique about the incident. Phantom or not, there was still a wild hyena wandering around our campsite at night ... this affirmed for me we were indeed camping in the heart of Africa. Secondly, it demonstrated the Masai are masters in their own environment, and there is no denying their courage.

Visit to a Masai Village

Early in the morning we boarded our safari truck, Ju Ju, as we again went searching for Africa's treasure of wildlife. As we drove along with side flaps rolled up, giving a totally unrestricted view, it seemed as if the wildlife was actually finding us: elephants, giraffes, gazelles; topis; wart hogs; secretary birds; guinea fowls; baboons; impalas; ostriches; the bastard bird that lays its eggs in the nests of other birds; hundreds of wildebeests; a thousand zebras. All seemed to fall voluntarily into the viewfinder of my camera, and I eagerly took their pictures. After having thus immersed ourselves in the endless myriad of exotic animals, we headed back to the campsite for lunch before our next activity.

After lunch we boarded *JuJu* again and headed to a local Masai village. It was in fact the village of our own Masai camp guards, which made this visit both special and authentic. When we arrived, we were met by some of the other local warriors who ushered us through a space in the protective thorny acacia brush, and into the centre of the Masai compound. We found ourselves standing on a soft ground-covering of manure, since this was where the cattle were brought at night for protection. Rectangular, dung-plastered huts stood at intervals in a circumference around this centre yard. Joining us in this centre circle, a line of brightly dressed and colourfully jeweled women began singing the welcoming song, followed by several other special choral selections all done in traditional style. The choral harmony of the women was unique, yet typically African. The singing concluded with the women forming a line and snaking around us, while they chanted and clapped. The men then began one of their traditional dances, effortlessly jumping high distances into the air, while one of the warriors who was draped in a lion mane headdress, blew into a large, twisted impala horn. The deep, low resonance from the horn echoed to the music of the women, and it was difficult not to think that this could have been happening in the same way a hundred years ago. There was no doubt our Masai entertainers were proud of their coveted songs and dances, and we were eager to have them share their traditions with us.

When the dancing concluded we were then invited into a Masai hut. Stooping to get through the doorway, my eyes had difficulty adjusting to the initial darkness, as my hand brushed against the hard dung-caked walls for balance. I went past the goat-room, turned left into a tunnel-type hallway, then made a right to enter the main room. This self-contained area had a fire pit, and a special enclave housing various containers such as the calabash gourd for the fresh blood and milk mixture. There was a second enclave for simple utensils and belongings, and also included a semi-enclosed area (still part of the main room) where we were told mama and papa slept. Although perhaps dubious of the building materials, Ikea would be hard pressed to be as practical and utilitarian in the efficient use of space. We were told that another impressive advantage of the structure was that there was no mortgage. It was also worthy of note that each hut is built in four months, and by the women only.

On our way back to camp we were fortunate to find a number of hippos soaking in the Mara River, which could be seen at close quarters. Near this location we also encountered four Kenyan game wardens dressed in the typical combat-style fatigues and carrying AK47 rifles to not only protect the animals from poachers, but also for personal safety on the Mara. With Karoma's influence, one warden volunteered to take us by foot along the riverbank to where he said a family herd of elephants was drinking. It turned out to be more wonderful African snapshot material, and we all returned to the campsite elated with the events of our day. Our Masai warriors were waiting for us by the fire. It would be another safe and secure night.

Balloons and Champagne on the Mara

It was a 5:00 am rising in order to be ready for the shuttle that took us to a rustic, but elegant lodge at Fig Tree Camp. It was here we would be launched in a hot air balloon to cross 20 kilometres of the Masai Mara. Arriving at the lodge, we completed our registration and payment, then downed a buffet breakfast and multiple cups of rich Kenyan coffee. With only a hint of light in the eastern sky, we were then escorted in the shadows to an open area where we could see hot orange flames gushing forcefully into two slowly inflating balloons. Each growing orb had attached to it a woven basket that held sixteen people. The baskets were tipped sideways on the ground, while the pilot continued pulling on a lever that blasted hot air from the flaming burner. Before the balloons lifted, we were required to crawl into the tipped basket, lay on our backs in a sitting position, and wait until our balloon began to rise.

We felt the balloon budge, and the basket jerked upright, allowing us to be in a standing position. Simultaneously we felt ourselves floating up in the semi-darkness. Except for the seemingly volcanic eruptions of the burners, everything else was silent and the dark ground quietly distanced itself beneath. As we rose smoothly into the sky, our attention was immediately drawn to the simultaneously rising red sun that ascended in slow motion behind us, casting a glow on the horizon. With just enough morning light now to see, there was a feeling of euphoria to be skimming over the grassy, brown plain far below. In the distance, we marveled at the immensity of the Masai Mara that continued to unravel and stretch all around. We could even see further into Tanzania, where this same plain became the even more immense Serengeti.

In this manner we floated effortlessly in the African sky, and our pilot began alternately ascending and descending to maximize our views at various heights. From a greater distance, animals appeared as slightly distinguishable dots, but when we floated closer to the ground their features became extraordinarily clear. At one point we spotted a huge solitary bull elephant at some distance. Targeting this magnificent beast, our pilot guided our balloon in for a closer look. Seeing us ominously appear from nowhere above, the bull elephant became quite vexed by our silent invasion. We continued to descend directly into his path, and the image of the angry elephant became larger and larger. I wondered if we were going to float into him. His powerful, massive body started shuffling back and forth aggressively as he flapped his ears wildly. We continued to advance directly toward him, and I could clearly see the white gleam from his threatening tusks. Suddenly, I felt a surge of heat with a blast from our burners, and our balloon swept over him. But the close encounter with this indignant bull had the pilot's desired effect of an adrenaline rush, and I felt a bit light headed with the excitement. It was an exhilarating feeling, and another precious 'stolen moment'.

As we continued our floating adventure, we marveled at the wildlife that came into view, only to disappear just as quickly behind and below us. It was a bit ironic to be, for once, looking down and not up at long-necked giraffes, feeding on seemingly miniature acacias. We spotted two lions resting on a dirt trail. From the balloon, they appeared to be harmless miniature domestic cats, resting leisurely on a ribbon of road that wound itself across the plain. Finally, after traveling over 20 kilometres across the Masai Mara, our pilot began our angled descent. He targeted an area near the Mara River where we would be able to view hippos and crocodiles on the ground, while we waited for our shuttle to retrieve us. Our basket skimmed upright across the ground before it came to rest. Still exhilarated by this unique and powerful experience, we jumped to the ground.

Our shuttles soon arrived and we climbed aboard for a short ride to a site where tables, covered in white linen and set with china, had already been arranged near a spreading acacia tree. Under the sunny sky in the middle of the Masai Mara, we would now be treated to a safari champagne breakfast. We were greeted by two waiters wearing white gloves and outfitted in smart looking scarlet tunics. Busy at the cooking table were two formally dressed chefs in white jackets and tall, white chef hats. Our entire group was overwhelmed with the whole wonderful experience and everyone chatted freely while enjoying individual omelets and the delicious buffet. Champagne glasses clinked in celebration of our safari balloon adventure. We would be leaving within the hour, but the marvelous breakfast served amidst the beauty and wilds of the Masai Mara seemed a fitting conclusion to a magical time- a fantasy fulfilled with many memorable moments. It was a stolen moment, and another item to cross off my 'bucket list.

More Magic on the Masai Mara (Photos)

Onto The Outskirts of Nairobi
In the District of Karen; Termite Appetizers; Exasperating e-Mail;
The Kuzuri Beads; Hugging Giraffes and Babying Elephants

Safari Day 14

In the District of Karen

Going north, we retraced our route from the Masai Mara back to the junction of the main highway that runs east west across Kenya, and continued onto Nairobi. About forty-five minutes outside of Nairobi we traveled through an area where the quality and value of both the land and buildings became clearly distinguishable. We were told many of the local Kenyans referred to this region as the 'white island', for obvious reasons. Before we reached Nairobi, Karoma turned off onto an alternate route to avoid much of the urban traffic, heading to a suburb called Karen. The district of Karen was named after an early white Kenyan pioneer, Karen Blixen, who was one of the main characters portrayed by Merryl Streep in the movie 'Out of Africa'. However, to reach this destination we first traveled through a number of less affluent Kikuyu villages, and also through a Masai village where people obviously knew Karoma and waved in recognition as we drove by.

By the time we reached the Karen district outside Nairobi, we were viewing manicured acreages with mansions set back from huge iron gates that had signs designating they were equipped with security alarms. On these premises there were often several surrounding buildings, many including a barn and paddock for the thoroughbred horses. This was obviously also predominantly a white area, in contrast to the other nearby regions through which we had traveled. Eventually the road we were on led us to a more western-style mall of several shops. These were accessed from both sides through large iron gates that had black security guards posted at the entrance and exit areas. Here we had a bit of time for some quick personal shopping before heading on to our campsite nearby. I stocked up on some South African wine, as well as bubble wrap to package two fragile, carved soapstone plates I had purchased along the way.

Termite Appetizers

Our campsite was a popular stopover for a number of the camping safari groups, and when we arrived, a few safari trucks were already parked and several tents erected nearby. The campsite had a small bar where one could socialize and even order a modest meal. In addition, there was a covered patio area outside. That evening, after the luxury of a hot shower, I decided to choose from the menu the peppersteak and chips that I would enjoy on the patio. Noticing it might start raining soon, I also ordered some wine and settled in under the patio canopy to await my meal.

It was a warm and somewhat humid evening, as the first scattered drops of rain began to fall. There was a dash to the tents to close flaps, zippers and check that the rain covers were secure. This was only the second storm we had experienced on the entire safari. By the time I got back to my wine, the light rain had changed to a deluge, but although a large volume of precipitation fell, the storm surprisingly spent itself quite quickly. However, after the rain there was an even more steamy, humid feel to the warm evening air.

Suddenly, out of nowhere, appeared swarms of flying insects about an inch and a half in length. Their disproportionately longer wings seemed to collectively produce a clicking symphony that filled the air, and although primarily attracted to the patio lights, the flying clouds were indiscriminant about where they landed, including all over us. I was informed that they were completely harmless termites, and that the warm evening temperature combined with the rainfall were the perfect conditions that stimulated the termites to leave their nests in thousands as part of their migration cycle. I was fascinated by this whole new experience, and as usual had multiple questions for Karoma about what was transpiring. As always, Karoma was most accommodating about sharing his vast knowledge and informed me that these insects were a popular food source for many Africans. He also mentioned that locals could anticipate when the termites would begin to swarm, and bags would be placed over termite mounds to collect thousands of them as they left the nest. These could then be eaten raw, or prepared in a dish. Karoma said he had done this as a boy.

Sipping on my third glass of wine, I playfully rebuked Karoma for trying to kid me. With a mischievous grin on his face, all of a sudden Karoma's arm shot out and his hand snatched a flying termite. He held the motionless insect by its wings, then looking directly at me, in slow motion he moved the body of the captured termite to his mouth, bit, chewed, and swallowed. Only the bodiless wings were left gripped between his two pinched fingers. I stared. Before I could recover from what I had just seen, another termite was grabbed in mid air and within seconds all that remained were the wings, while Karoma chewed and smiled. For one of the first times on the safari I was completely speechless, and hurriedly grabbed at my fourth glass of wine. In the interval of still trying to comprehend what had just happened, Karoma repeated the action while nonchalantly telling me it tasted quite good, with a flavour similar to peanut butter.

By now Karoma had attracted a small audience of safari campers, all equally as fascinated by the whole spectacle. Each time Karoma munched on a termite, a few young women nearby displayed some revulsion, and contorted their faces. And each time Karoma swallowed, I believe I took another swallow of wine. This, in turn, produced its own consequences. I foolishly thought I could not let Karoma have such unanswered satisfaction at shocking this 'mzungu'.

Motion before mind, my hand shot into the still swarming cloud before me, and I found myself staring at the insect I was holding by the wings. Imitating Karoma, I advanced this apparent delicacy to my mouth, bared my teeth, bit ... and became vaguely aware of crunchiness. I could not detect the peanut butter taste that had in part tempted me to try this tidbit treat, and in fact found the crispy creature to be rather bland in flavour. Yet it was not unpleasant. The wine no doubt reinforced the sense of dare I felt with a smiling Karoma seated nearby, and soon I was repeatedly snatching the flying morsels from the air and biting the bodies off the wings, calling them my scrumptious appetizers. I must admit, in this temporary state of perversion I was also enjoying the squirming reaction from other safari groups drinking on the patio. Appetizers consumed, my peppersteak and chips finally arrived. To a confused waiter, I strongly recommended putting fresh termite appetizers on the menu. However, in the morning I found the waiter from the previous evening sweeping up piles of dead termites from the patio. Looking at the piles of lifeless insects, I decided not to remind him about my recommendation for the menu. They had lost last night's appeal.

Exasperating e-Mail
Having had rain the night before, packing up our tents and gear was a wetter operation than previously experienced, but as always with our safari group, no one seemed to mind. Our busy day would include a number of activities, including a brief stop back at the mall in the Karen district, and then we would be on our way to the Kenyan-Tanzanian border. I headed straight for an internet café I had spotted on our previous visit. E-mailing from Africa is not always an easy process, and with sparse internet locations in East Africa I was well overdue to contact family and friends back home. Although it took almost one third of my paid time to get logged on, I typed solidly for fifty minutes and was able to share a few updated stories and adventures from our safari.

The old antique computer at my station was extremely slow, as were most I had used in East Africa. I was also struggling to read what I was writing because the monitor screen displayed only part of the text, and much of that was barely legible. I could have taken the time to try to make some monitor adjustments, but we only had a short stop in Karen and I was desperate to complete my message within the time frame. On the positive side, I was appreciative that the chair on which I sat was firmly fixed to its legs, that the room was adequately lit, and that the keyboard appeared clean and free from grime. At one of the internet sites I had used in Arushu, the seat was not secured to the legs and it kept slipping off. They were also trying to save electricity, and only the glow from the monitors lit the room, which left me stumbling to find my way to the assigned station. En route I almost knocked over several nearby computers and smashed into the chair with the unattached seat, sending it flying across the room. Also, in many of the sites the keyboards were so dirty and grimy that eventually I started carrying packages of wet-napkins to sanitize my hands after using the computer.

Knowing I only had minutes left before our safari truck, *JuJu*, would be leaving Karen, I quickly finished my e-mail but decided to click on the spell check before sending it. To my shock, like magic, the whole text on the screen completely disappeared ... the screen was entirely blank. I tried in vain to recapture what I had already written, but the computer would not cooperate. Finally, with no other option, I explained to the attending technician that I had lost my message when I attempted a spell check. Without seeking my approval, she immediately grabbed the mouse and closed the document. I knew instantly my e-mail was now gone forever. I was devastated, particularly since I knew our safari truck would by now be waiting for me. The final indignity was that the attendant would not discount any of the computer time charges for what was the cafe's own technical malfunction. With neither time to argue nor negotiate, I paid and left running. Although my exasperating e-mail experience initially left me a bit distraught, on my way back to the truck I remembered some important acronyms I had learned on safari that allowed me to put my electronic saga into the African context. Two of these were: AWA (Africa Wins Again) and TIA (This Is Africa). Feeling better, as I climbed the stairs into the vehicle, I whispered the other Swahili expression I had recently learned, "Hakuna Matta" (No worries).

The Kuzuri Beads
One of the side tours near Nairobi that was anticipated would appeal to the general interest of our group, was a visit to a neatly kept compound which serves as a factory where single or abandoned mothers work in a cooperative environment to produce beautiful handcrafted ceramic beads. Not only did many of us leave the Kuzuri Bead Factory with purchases of the colourful necklaces that have become internationally renowned, but I believe all of us were touched with its story exemplifying the human value and integrity which is associated with its success.
The project was originally conceived and implemented by Lady Susan Wood, who with her husband originated the East African Flying Doctor Service. Susan originally started the bead manufacturing with two single mothers, but soon realized that there were more mothers who needed a source of income that would assist in providing an education for their children. Eventually in 1988, the small shed in which she first produced the beads progressed to a new factory on the famous Karen Blixen Estate- Karen, of course, being more popularly associated with the film, 'Out of Africa'. Today the factory has grown to provide employment to as many as one hundred twenty mothers. The name Kuzuri is Swahili for "small and beautiful", which also symbolically speaks of the children and their mothers who are the focus of the enterprise.

Our group was affably met by a guide who gave us a thorough tour of the factory, starting from where the mothers first mould the beads from clay, then through the processes of glazing, kiln baking and hand painting, to the final stringing of the beads into unique, colourful necklaces. Our presence in the factory was welcomed by the women who sat at long tables, often chatting to each other while they worked. They smiled and waved at us as we wandered among them, and were eager to show us what they were doing. As I climbed back onto *JuJu* to go to our next destination, I appreciated having seen this commendable and praiseworthy project first hand, and was proud to have purchased quality gifts for my partner and two daughters back home.

Hugging Giraffes and Babying Elephants
Before we left the Nairobi area for the Tanzanian border, we had two additional activities on our list: (1) a visit to the Langatta Giraffe Centre; and (2) a stop at an animal orphanage that specializes primarily in the rescue and rehabilitation of baby elephants.

The Langatta Giraffe Centre has proved to be a tremendously popular destination for both tourists and locals alike. Here one is not only able to view the giraffes at very close quarters, but standing on a circular platform you can actually feed the giraffes at their own height. The platform surrounds an interior building that also functions as the centre, and which has office and display rooms as well as an amphitheatre. The Giraffe Centre is actually 'The

African Fund for Endangered Wildlife Kenya' (A.F.E.W.Kenya), a nonprofit and nongovernmental organization dedicated to saving the endangered Rothschild Giraffe. This species of giraffe lost its natural habitat in Western Kenya due to encroaching agriculture, with the result that it is estimated only about 130 are left in the world. In addition to conservation, the Giraffe Centre also provides free environmental education to youth, and to the adults like us who visit the centre.

When we climbed the steps to the balcony-style platform, a uniformed attendant was distributing food pellets from a watering pail to allow visitors to feed the giraffes. The giraffes knew the routine well, and ambled up to the platform to patiently receive their treats. At first it was a bit disconcerting to have this huge head, over one third one's own body size, move toward your hand. The second more astounding thing was to see an enormously long, pointed tongue, over half the length of your arm, slip out to slurp up the pellets. It took some more nervous visitors several tries to mount enough courage to be able to feed a giraffe, but their concerns were ill founded for the giraffes acted quite respectfully. For those quite comfortable with this wondrous animal, a more challenging and entertaining method of feeding the pellet was to hold it between one's teeth and let the long tongue pluck it right out of your mouth, like a giraffe delicately plucking an acacia leaf from among sharp thorns... or giving an inadvertent kiss! As for me, standing on the platform at head height to the giraffe, I held a few pellets in the palm of my hand. As the giraffe's head approached, I then slowly moved the pellets away to encourage it to get as close as possible. Soon I had one arm around a tolerantly feeding giraffe, enjoying hugging and stroking it and leaving no doubt as to my affection for these animals. I rubbed its fur-covered, knobby horns and felt the small, darker tufts of hair at the end of them. I scratched its long extending, creamy-white ears. The short mane on the back of its neck felt bristly, and I rubbed part of its accessible neck, just under its elongated head that was now partly resting on my chest. The pointed pink tongue emerged from its mouth and I felt a tickle on the inside of my hand as it found the pellets. When the giraffe had finished feeding it was understandably not as motivated to continue its relationship with me, and moved to another awaiting food source. But I had already enjoyed a 'stolen moment' with my giraffe, a moment admittedly not without awe and emotional impact.

Following the feeding, our group entered the amphitheatre to attend a very informative presentation on the plight of the giraffe and about the worthwhile work the Lengatta Giraffe Centre does in Africa. The mini-lecture helped us to identify the three species of giraffe, and gave a useful context for many things we had already observed about giraffes on our safari. The modest entry fee already covered in our safari cost helps to support the centre, and I left knowing we had in some small way contributed to a very important ecological cause.

Babying Elephants

The next stop was also at an animal refuge, but this time it was a visit to an orphanage specializing in baby elephants. It is now called the Daphne Sheldrick's Elephant Orphanage, the name being changed after the death of her husband, David. Although their work is ongoing, the focus for the public who enter the park by donation is during a restricted fixed feeding that takes place daily from 11:00 am to noon. The park is too small to support adult elephants, but young elephants ranging from a few months to three years are given refuge here, with the intent of preparing them for reintegration into the wild when they are ready. There are a variety of reasons why these young elephants might have been brought here from any part of Kenya: the mothers having been killed by poachers; the natural death of a mother; or the abandonment of the baby for other reasons.

When we arrived, only about thirty people were in attendance, which allowed us to get very close to the elephants. Only a single large rope separated the various-sized young ones from the visitors, but like children this did not prevent the babies from reaching over with their leathery, bristly-haired trunks to make contact with the onlookers. I couldn't resist feeling one of the baby trunks as it explored around my hand and even up part of my arm. The attendants were very tolerant of this, which promoted bonding and affection on both sides.

The antics of the sprite elephants were hilarious, as they interacted with their attendant feeders and bathed in the attention of the spectators. When the little elephants were satisfied from feeding, again like children, they sought amusement and attention elsewhere. One larger young one could not resist exploring in the crowd itself, and simply and innocently went through the rope barrier to go give personal greetings to a surprised group of people. Although understandably some quickly moved away from this over-rambunctious mass coming enthusiastically toward them, a few others rushed to try to give the baby a rub or a pat. It was all great fun as the attendants reprimanded this precocious infant behaviour, and struggled to pull the resisting baby back on the other side of the rope. At the same time, two or three other babies were amusing themselves, pushing an inflated ball around in a puddle of water with their trunks or feet. Every once in a while one of them would stop the play, then decide to spray some muddy water all over, including in the crowd, then continue playing again.

It was impossible not to enjoy this special interaction, even though we were all aware of the circumstances that had brought them here. However, the work being accomplished at this elephant orphanage is impressive, and gives reason for optimism. It was amazing to learn that ongoing support for their re-integration may continue up to 5 years after the elephants have been relocated to a natural environment. Trauma has often played a significant part in their separation from their mothers and families, and as such rehabilitation must take this into account. As with the Giraffe Centre, one had very positive feelings about being able to view the elephants in this manner, and particularly to know that in some small way our presence supports the cause. As we left to re-board *JuJu* to continue our journey to the Tanzanian border, I looked back to see the small playful elephants running around each other and wielding their undeveloped, stubby trunks in mischief. I realized that Africa's powerful images can come in a variety of settings, even at a baby elephant refuge.

Onto the Ngorongoro Crater Area
A Curdling Scream; Passing Through Arushu; To Kudu Lodge and Campsite

Safari Day 15

A Curdling Scream

Leaving the elephant orphanage, Karoma once again avoided driving through the Nairobi traffic, thereby hoping to shave off up to two hours traveling time to our next campsite. Soon we were back into the semi-arid landscape of the Rift Valley, with its flat-topped acacia trees and dry, rocky terrain. It reminded me of the Lake Baringo area where wandering goats replaced cattle as the dominant domestic animal.

With the side flaps of *JuJu* rolled up, and a warm breeze blowing into the vehicle, we seemed to be making good time despite the frequent potholes on the narrow two-lane highway that caused Karoma to adjust speed and gear down from time to time. We had already had a full day of activities and everyone was content to relax and take in the scenery. In this restful state, suddenly we were startled by a loud blast of air on the driver's side, as a very large commercial truck roared by us at an incredibly excessive speed. Simultaneously we heard a loud scream, a penetrating noise that was blood curdling in its volume and high pitch. I instantly thought someone walking on the highway must have been hit, and perhaps someone had screamed.

Karoma immediately slowed our vehicle and pulled over to the side of the road. The commercial truck tore on ahead of us, not even adjusting its speed. Just after the unsettling scream, those passengers on the right hand side who were looking out the open flaps gasped as they saw the corpse of a donkey lying at the side of the road. Also at the same time as the scream, I had seen something go flying across the front of our truck. This turned out to be a second donkey. Apparently the seemingly run-away truck had struck the donkeys as it was overtaking us at high speed, and had scattered the two of them in opposite directions like pins flying from the smash of a bowling ball. Our cook, who was riding with us, was very upset at what had happened, and angrily criticized the speeding driver for his recklessness and lack of care for livestock. But he was particularly upset at the way the truck had dangerously passed us, and that he did not stop.

When we continued on our way, we spotted the truck ahead of us at the side of the road. The vehicle had finally stopped, but not out of concern for the donkeys, nor for our safety, but rather only to inspect the damage to his own truck. Karoma again pulled over and stopped, while John immediately jumped out of *JuJu* and quickly walked back to the commercial truck, all the while admonishing him and telling him he had to compensate the owner for his dead donkeys. Of equal concern was the fact that the donkey sent flying across the front of our safari truck could have hit us, and it was very upsetting to think of what might have happened then. At the next police check, common at intervals along the highway, Karoma reported the incident and gave the license number of the other vehicle. It was obvious to us that in Africa where livestock and other indigenous animals are always on the road, it was imperative to drive accordingly. We also knew that it was in part a credit to Karoma's own focus on safety and care in driving, that we had not been part of a more serious accident. But the sound of that scream, like what might come from a person, echoed in my mind for some considerable time and distance after the incident.

That evening I was ready for an early retirement to my tent. I knew we had to be up at 5:30 the next morning for a long haul to our campsite on the other side of Arushu, and into the country of the famed Mount Kilimanjaro. Climbing 'Kili' is on my 'Bucket List', and I was looking forward to my very first peek at this African icon, if the weather permitted.

Passing through Arushu

The early morning start was in part so that we would be prepared for any potential long delays we might experience in crossing the border from Kenya into Tanzania. Realizing from when we had passed over the western Ugandan-

Kenyan border how complicated and time consuming such crossings can be, we were all supportive of leaving early. When we arrived at the border we followed the routine of giving our passports to Tasha, who then handled all the bureaucracy while we remained aboard *JuJu*. Although two of the officials who were supposed to process our documentation for entry visas arrived at work a half hour late, we were grateful that Tasha was able to take care of business on our behalf, with only that much delay. Her experience in dealing with these matters was an advantage on our entire safari expedition.

Once across the border we threaded past the usual string of commercial huts and shops typical of border villages, but soon we were back into the arid region of the Rift Valley. A few Masai structures sprang up along the road, but these were now more sparse. I observed that their construction was also changing from the dung-plastered exteriors to that of stone blocks. After a time we began a gradual climb which most always meant an increase in precipitation. The greenery and the amount of cultivated land began to appear more frequently. Although the climb was subtle, we were soon in a thickening mist, which unfortunately meant I would not get the view of Mount Kilimanjaro for which I had hoped. I knew nevertheless we were very close to Arushu, the destination city for climbers to the renowned white-capped mountain.

Approaching Arushu from the north, the outskirts hinted at a thriving economy. This was reinforced by its larger buildings, including a modern blue-glassed high-rise that looked very attractive. At a nearby intersection was a traffic light, something rarely seen to date on our journey, and for some bizarre reason this seemed to create quite a bit of excitement among us all. There was just something a bit perverse about traveling all the way to Africa to become excited by a traffic light in Arushu. Perhaps it was that the small city in general appeared more modern than larger centres we had visited to date. After some time in town to exchange currency, on the other side of Arushu we made another short stop at a super market named Shop Rite. I reflected that this must be a modern city, for the super market even utilized the North American slang spelling in its name.

In the store I located the shelves stocked with beer, only to find I had an important decision to make. In Uganda I drank the local 'Nile' beer. In Kenya I switched to the local 'Tusker' beer. Tusker was to date my favourite, and I was reluctant not to make this my purchase. But here the local beer was fittingly called 'Kilimanjaro', a name that inspired me. What was one to do? Tusker ... Kilimanjaro? Tusker ... Kilimanjaro? We only had a very short interval before we continued on our journey, and I did not have much time to ponder this crucial mystery. I quickly grabbed a six-pack of Tusker, and a six-pack of Kilimanjaro, and headed for the checkout.

To Kudu Lodge and Campsite

Leaving Arushu we passed a couple of smaller coffee plantations near the Kilimanjaro International Airport. Further south, we were back in the typically brown plain of the Rift Valley. After about two hours we turned east to head into the hills of a more mountainous region. The highway here was very impressive by any standards. The high quality paved road with its yellow lined shoulders, as well as the bridges and accompanying drainage system and infrastructure, were apparently built and subsidized by the Chinese during Tanzania's socialist era. This was the best road we had seen in all of East Africa. We were on our way to the highly desired tourist destination of the Ngorongoro Crater, famous for its African wildlife situated deep on the bottom floor of the crater itself.

Not only the road, but also the quality of the shops, houses and buildings began to improve. The increasing numbers of curio shops were often painted with zebra stripes or other Masai designs, making them colourful and appealing. There were a greater number of streams and rivulets here, and the area had an abundance of water. Small banana groves became commonplace. Continuing to ascend, we had an expansive view both of the Rift Valley below, and of the large and scenic Lake Manyara that shared this vista. At this altitude, abundant crops thrived on the fertile, volcanic soil. About two kilometres past the village of Karatu, we finally arrived at our campsite where we would stay the night before going on to the Ngorongoro Crater. Kudu, the name of the lodge and campsite, is relatively modern, with ongoing expansion. Here we found a 60-seat restaurant, a bar with a satellite television, an activity room and an outdoor garden area that frequently has local drummers, dancers and acrobats performing for the guests. It also had an internet café.

For some time during the day I had been thinking of the hot shower I would take when we got to the campsite, especially since the last two showers had been only quick, cold rinses. The shower stall here seemed relatively clean, so in preparation for this luxury I organized my soap and towel for easy access, slipped off my clothes and entered the shower expectantly. Turning on the tap, I waited for the blast of hot water ... nothing ... not even a dribble. I tried the other tap, then frantically began turning both taps on and off at the same time ... nothing. Then I heard someone yell into the shower facility that there was a problem with the water line, and my hopes for a warm cleansing soak were shattered. By now I knew that in Africa the simplest things taken for granted should not be taken so, and I found myself again mumbling the acronym "TIA" (This Is Africa). Suddenly I remembered that in Arushu I had purchased the new Tanzanian beer, Kilimanjaro. This was a perfect time to sample it, and for now would be an acceptable alternative to a hot shower.

Although several in our safari group planned to attend the music and dancing that would take place in the outdoor lodge gardens that evening, it would be one of the only events of the entire safari that I would forego. I had decided to brave the internet and try to send a few messages. I also planned to catch up on the shower that had eluded me earlier. It had been a full day, and knowing we would be up at 5:15 the next morning I wanted to be well rested for my anticipated adventure into the bowels of the Ngorongoro Crater. Retiring early to my tent I quickly fell asleep to the rhythm of the African drums that echoed from the lodge gardens- a fitting conclusion to another African safari day.

Into The Bowels Of The Crater
To the Rim; On the Crater Floor; Finding Felines;
The Lakes And the River; Leaving Ngorongoro

Safari Day 16

To The Rim

Because it would not be possible or practical for our large safari truck to make the steep ascents and descents required for the Ngorongoro Crater, a jeep and minibus arrived as our transportation for this part of the safari. The 40 kilometre ride to the park gate took us through several villages and past dense agricultural lands positioned on mountainsides, or nestled in rolling hills. En route we saw people walking, riding bikes or sharing transportation in open vehicles jammed with passengers. Eventually we reached the Loduare Gate, and we began our winding ascent into the morning mist that gave a smoky effect to the landscape.

As we climbed, the bumpy, narrow road took us through a dense cloud forest crowded with immense fig and pillarwood trees. These tall growing structures contributed to a thick, verdant canopy. Masses of moss added a carpet-like appearance to the looming, leafy timbers. The boughs of the giant trees in turn supported other rich growth such as the Old Man's Beard lichen that hung in clumps. Dense underbrush, consisting of large ferns and other lush vegetation, combined to create a sense of mystery and mystique. Around each sharp bend, steep drop-offs formed green gorges that sank below and out of sight. In this way, the landscape was totally distinct from the surrounding countryside.

Passing through this unique area we finally reached the rim of the crater, then continued to circumnavigate along the top of it. Though the lingering mist was now disappearing, both it and the angle of our location still prevented us from having a clear view of the inner crater, but we knew it was off to our right. The surroundings became more sparse, and we passed several branch roads that led to a variety of tourist lodges that had been built at various locations around the crater's inner edge. Finally traversing a steep mini-crater, we abruptly arrived at a place where 600 dizzy metres below, we gazed out onto an enormous bowl- the Ngorongoro Crater. We had come upon it so suddenly and unexpectedly, that its vacuous vista came as a shock, enhancing and enriching the wonder of the view that lay before us.

The enormous crater stretched off into the distance, to the blue-gray edge of the opposite wall on the far side. The crater, in fact, spans a distance of almost 20 kilometres and covers over 265 sq. km. Ngorongoro was once a huge volcano, thought to date back about 2,500,000 years. It is believed to have been caused after a large major eruption. This, in turn, caused its lava cone to collapse inward, leaving intact what is known as the caldera. Over time this crater has come to be the home of over 30,000 animals.

I stood in silence and gazed out over the circular expanse. Off to one side in the crater was the outline of a distant blue soda lake. With my telephoto lens I could faintly detect dark, thread-like lines and miniscule dots near the lake. The lines turned out to be wildebeests indiscriminately following one another until, for no reason, there was a change in direction, and a new thread would be formed. The dots became the prolific variety of game we would later encounter. I was excited to get below, but it was with a little trepidation that I looked at the dusty ribbon that snaked its way down the inner crater wall. This was the road we had to take down. Descending would be an adventure in itself.

My view from the rim

On The Crater Floor
Climbing back into our vehicles, we plunged over the lip of the crater and began our descent. The road was steep and hazardous, and we hung onto whatever we could in the vehicle as we crept down the rocky, bumpy and dusty road into the bowels of the Ngorongoro. With some relief we finally reached the flat bottom of the crater, and immediately found ourselves in the thick of a community of mixed wildebeests and zebras. We did not have to travel long to discover they were scattered absolutely everywhere ... some marching in lines ... some running, walking, standing, grazing ... multiple herds of these animals blending or separating from one another in continuous sequence. It was the Africa we vaguely knew from documentaries and movies, but now we were in the midst of it and its impact was overwhelming. There was no wrong way to look. Every degree of the unfolding circle of scenery unveiled another mass of animals. However, we also discovered that such magic moments must come at a price, and that cost was being able to survive the challenge of riding the rough, dusty roads of the Ngorongoro.

Our two vehicles bumped, jumped and swerved along trails that quickly filled with rolling clouds of dust that continually, and sometimes entirely, engulfed us. A persistent cool, but not unwelcome, breeze blew across the crater plain, and if you faced the right direction it eased the choking dust somewhat. However, although uncomfortable we recognized we were blessed with the gift of the Ngorongoro all around us, and we quietly did what was necessary to adapt. After all, a safari in the Ngorongoro Crater was not something to be missed. We looked, spotted, stopped, clicked, watched, marveled, moved on, and then started looking again. Everyone contributed to the adventure. Someone would spot a hyena and call out, others pointed at ostriches or warthogs, egrets and eagles, and of course there were always the wildebeests and zebras. Even for the density of wildlife, it was still a huge area to explore, and we were determined to accomplish as much of this as we could.

At one point Karoma pulled the jeep over and we popped off three sections of the roof. We could now stand and view 360 degrees ... that is if you were adept at bouncing, swaying and being thrown around while hanging onto your camera with one hand, and onto the vehicle with the other. And so it went, sweeping the crater in our vehicles as we soaked up the scenery of gazelles, bastard birds, crown cranes, jackals and an ongoing and seemingly endless inventory of wildlife. It seemed nothing could become repetitive. However, just when one thought that they had seen everything the day would bring, Karoma spotted a special figure in the distance. I was ecstatic.

Finding Felines

We were told that sighting cheetahs in the Ngorongoro would be more rare than viewing many of the other animals here. But with his keen eyesight and experience, Karoma amazingly had picked out a princely cheetah sitting erect in the brown grass, blending in perfectly with its setting. With such masterful camouflage, I realized even the most careful of its prey would have difficulty detecting its presence. Even though the distance was further than one would have preferred, through the telephoto lens I could clearly appreciate its sleekness and beauty. It looked both independent and contemplative as it sat motionless, scanning the horizon of its territory. I thought whimsically perhaps it was focusing on the beauty of its surroundings ... but more probably it was considering what it might prefer for supper. For some time no one spoke a word, all quietly internalizing the magic of the moment, but eventually it was time to move on, and with a cloud of dust following the vehicle, our cheetah disappeared in the distance.

We had not traveled far before we found ourselves approaching another feline, in fact two ... both a male and female lion. I recalled that I had learned that the isolation of the Crater, with its abundant food source, had influenced the genetics of the local lions, with the result that they were generally bigger than other African lions. Although they continued to grow in numbers, at one point their population dwindled suddenly. It was discovered they were being menaced by a fly that resulted in some deaths, and many subsequently abandoned the crater. Although their population has again stabilized, there remains cause for concern that a similar thing could happen again. To complicate this, inbreeding has also become a concern due the fewer mating options. This whole circumstance made seeing these two lions very special to me.

Our jeep edged up to some other stationary vehicles, and the engine was turned off. The male and female were laying about 15 to 20 metres away in the deeper grass. Even though very large, it was amazing to see how well they blended into their surroundings. Then suddenly the male stood, as if to keep watch over the female. As I zoomed in with my telephoto lens, the male looked directly toward us and began methodically walking in our direction, coming closer with each padded step. I kept adjusting my lens to compensate for the decreasing distance, but within minutes he was directly beside our jeep, and beneath me. In fact, this magnificent beast was so close I could no longer take photos with the larger lens. Just as I considered changing lenses, I heard Karoma's coaching voice repeating at intervals in low, quiet tones, "Don't make any sudden movements ... Don't make any sudden movements ... Don't make any sudden movements".

In point of fact I was so mesmerized with the lion being this close, I couldn't have moved anyway. I could feel my accelerated heartbeat, and could hear myself breathe. I dared not move, and just stared at this African icon standing regally below me. I could see the heaving of its enormous chest as it breathed, and even noted how the darker coloured, straggly strands of its mane appeared beauty-parlour streaked with yellow and blond highlights. Totally absorbed in the moment, it even occurred to me that if I leaned a bit more, I could even run my fingers through that coarse, shaggy hair. Then the spell was broken as I again heard Karoma's soft voice, "Don't make any sudden movements". Eventually the king wandered back to its female, placing their images once again in the focus of my lens, and I 'clicked'. Instantly I knew I had just experienced another one of those rare 'stolen moments' that I would revisit many times. For a second, Africa had once again unveiled her heart.

The Lakes And The River
We continued combing the crater, crisscrossing a maze of trails leading us to different areas that held concentrations of different kinds of wildlife. Of course there were always the wildebeests and zebras everywhere. Our route finally took us near the main lake. Approaching from a distance we could first see what appeared to be pink painted lines streaked across the water. But closer to the lake, these formations transformed into patches and

blotches of standing, swimming and flying flamingoes. It reminded me of the apple blossom orchards back home in the Okanagan in the spring, a blending of white and pink everywhere. The vista of the lake, reflecting a pallet of pink and blue colours, became especially rich when viewed with the silhouettes of the buffalo walking or running on the shore. It was as if we were wandering in an African art gallery of nature. Each colorful scene was a painting, and the distant crater walls were the frames.

On another area of the crater, and fortunately by this time near a washroom outpost, we found a smaller lake we had not seen from up on top. The lake was edged on one side by a mass of green rushes and a few trees. The tops of large rocks appeared to be above the surface of the water, but these were in fact the heads of hippos whose bodies were hidden in the water, out of the hot African sun. The lake, with its hippos, was picturesque and worthy of more photos, and added to the wonderment of the day.

Knowing our time in the crater was almost up, we proceeded to a small winding river that held just enough water to support a crowd of hippos. They huddled close together to make maximum use of the small space, sometimes only their backs appearing above the water, other times their heads draped over another hippo. In rotation, their short tails vibrated at an accelerated rate to not only scatter the dung, a sort of built in manure spreader, but also to splash water on their sun-sensitive backs. Grunting noises emanated from them from time to time, otherwise they were content to minimize motion during this hot time of the day.

Birds walking on the backs of hippos

Leaving Ngorongoro

As well as the viewing of wildlife and scenery, it is said that the mark of a very successful safari adventure is having been able to feel and taste the experience as well. This being the case, I must have had a very successful safari experience, for my throat and lungs were choked with dust, and dust seemed to be all I could taste and feel. I calculated I had either eaten, or now wore, half the crater. My clothes and camera were totally covered in a film of fine powder. My socks had completely changed colour and there were new dark patterns on my shirt and shorts that had miraculously appeared over the past few hours. There certainly would be some challenges getting everything clean, including myself. However, the exhilaration of actually having been in the bowels of Ngorongoro Crater, and having so indulged in the visuals of its wildlife and scenery, seemed to make the dust a small inconvenience.

We began to make our way toward the crater wall where we would then climb back to the rim. However, since it was a one-way traffic pattern for going in and coming out of the crater, we would be leaving by a different route. It was one that took us by a lone elephant feeding on long grass in a marshy area, the last animal we would see before leaving. We began our ascent up the inner crater wall to the rim, and again found ourselves on a steep switchback road of an even steeper grade than the trail by which we had originally entered. For those not focusing on the drop-offs that accompanied each switchback turn, the vista of the circular world we were leaving below was ever changing. As we climbed higher, the dryness of the plain was suddenly replaced by lush vegetation.

At the top of the rim, at a viewpoint where we stopped, I pensively looked down into the distant circumference below. I knew that something had happened to me down there, but found it hard to put into context. It seemed to be something mystical, I didn't actually know. But what I did know was that I would leave Africa different than when I arrived … and for now that was both satisfying and consoling.

At Arushu Masai Camp
Tanzanite Tales; Visit to the Chemists; Cattle and Camels

Safari Days 17-18

After Ngorongoro, we had driven to a campsite about 20 kilometres outside of Arushu. I awoke at 6:30 the next morning and peeked outside my tent flap. The breaking light exposed the shadowy movement of a dozen or so plump guinea fowl that were feeding and darting about. This seemed like a great start to a new day, and I was further pleased to have finally mastered the use of my mosquito net, without again wrapping myself up in it. With its pyramid shape, where one plane of the net was to stretch over your sleeping body, I had finally learned to tuck all the edges under the sides of my foam mattress in just the right proportions, with suitable space for my head and shoulders. Having frequently awoken in the morning all tangled up, I had projected it would be more embarrassing to be discovered in my tent choked by my own mosquito net, than more romantically to have been dragged off by a lion or wild hyena in the middle of the night. I concluded my safari skills were definitely progressing.

To get an early start to the day, I decided to brave a cold shower and again attempt to get the Ngorongoro Crater dust out of my clothes by taking them into the shower with me, and stomping on them while I showered. I had already hand-washed this laundry twice, but each time the rinse water was still shockingly dirty. We would be making a return trip to Arushu later in the morning, and I wanted to be able to walk around the town without creating dust clouds as I moved. I rationalized that stomping on my laundry was not that far off the African way of beating clothes against the rocks, and I got a shower thrown in at the same time. It seemed like good safari-time management to me.

My agenda in Arushu would be to change some currency, attempt some e-mail, and then check out the indigenous Tanzanite gems. If the gems were of good quality and the price also affordable, my plan was to buy the stones as gifts, and have them set into jewelry back home.

Tanzanite Tales

After dealing with the usual challenges of African e-mail, I immersed myself in the busy flow of Arushu's pedestrian traffic and negotiated my way along the main street through town. By now I had become almost immune to the occasional hocker who easily identified me as a Mzungu (white tourist), and tried to stuff into my hands anything from CD's to carvings to postcards to sunglasses. They were now more easily ignored, but I could not ignore what for me was still the novelty of seeing the occasional woman I passed, carrying a heavy load on her head. Even in a more urban setting it was a reminder that this was Africa.

I found the small gem shop located in the Arushu Hotel. It had been recommended to me by Tasha because it was noted for its certified, quality tanzanite gems, and I was told others on safari in the past had been pleased with their purchases. This gem is unique in that it is found nowhere else in the world except in Tanzania, and in its raw form it is heated to a specific temperature for a specific period of time to produce the beautiful shades of purple-blue characteristic of the stone. The gems range in shades of blue, however the deeper and clearer the blue apparently the higher the quality of the gem.

When I arrived at the hotel I mistakenly entered from the back and had to inquire as to the location of the dealership, called Swala Gems. I was redirected next door. I later became aware that another person from our own safari group, in her Kiwi accent, had similarly asked a bellhop about the shop's location. However, when she followed the directions that had been given, she ended up in the hotel "gym", not at the gem shop. I wondered how many misunderstandings I had been responsible for with my Canuck accent.

I found that the proprietor, whose name was Mark, was very helpful and professional. I made it clear my purchase would be a modest amount, but he did not mind what I chose to spend, and began showing me various gems within my designated price range. As he helpfully explained a bit about the tanzanite stones, he also began relating a recent story of a young couple that had met on a safari and became engaged. Though he hardly had any money left, the fiancé brought his girl to the gem shop to see if he could buy for her a very tiny tanzanite stone. As it turned out, the fiancé had only $43 American to spend, but Mark set about trying to find a tanzanite sparkle that he could sell to them for that price. Mark said that he at last succeeded in finding something for them, but chuckled he wondered how long the relationship was going to last if this splurge was an indication of what was to come. Enjoying the story, I replied that I very much wanted my relationship to last longer than what the young lad might expect of his, so told him we would up the price a bit.

Mark set several trays on the desk for me to inspect, and humorously said we would try to find one that should give me at least a few years of marriage. As I left the shop, I was excited with my purchases, anticipating the positive responses they would receive as gifts back home.

Visit To The Chemists

Before we left Arushu to return to our campsite, it had been recommended that since four of us from the safari had been tumultuously submerged in the Nile during white water rafting, we should as a precaution purchase the medication Praziquantel. This would address any possible worm-associated infection to which we may have been exposed. It was pointed out that the same medication back home was expensive, and could cost up to $60, while here in Arushu it would be much cheaper.

In Arushu, a pharmacy or drug store is known as the 'Chemists', the pharmacist being of course the chemist. Once I understood the language, and who I was supposed to see and where I was supposed to go, I headed off to buy my precautionary drugs. It must have been amusing for the chemist, because all four of us arrived at short intervals from one another, with me coming through the door last. Each in turn ordered the exact same thing, but because we did not arrive at the same time there was no apparent connection at first. However, all crowded in the small shop at the same time, one by one he took the same order and then individually filled the same prescription. The chemist began to look rather suspicious by the third identical order. Finally, when it was my turn to parrot the request, he finally asked if we knew each other, and had we fallen out of the same boat? We confessed.

There was the option of taking the medication now, or as recommended by the Chemist, to wait and see if we developed any of the symptoms indicating we were infected. He said if we did not need the drugs, we could save them for another time. As for saving the drugs for another time, I wasn't certain when I might again be going for a dip in the Nile, nor in any other African river having a similar risk of infection. However, I decided to wait anyway. To date I now still have my small packet of 5 tablets in my medicine cabinet at home, awaiting my next dunk in the Nile. As for the cost, it indeed was good advice to make our purchase in Arushu instead of making the $60 purchase back home. At the chemists, the medication came to $2,500 TS (Tanzanian shillings), the equivalent of $2.50.

Cattle and Camels

With so many kilometres to travel and places to visit on our safari, we did not have many opportunities to remain long in the same campsite. Although I was always excited to be moving on to new scenery or the next adventure, occasionally it felt good to be able to remain in a campsite an extra day and to have a bit more time to do a few personal things. That might be reading, writing in the travelogue, exploring around the campsite or lodging, or just taking care of laundry. It was also a small break from packing up one's things and taking down the tent, and from traveling longer distances in *JuJu*. As a result, I was pleased to be returning to the Arushu Masai Camp, and already planned to do a couple of things while there. First, Tasha and Karoma had planned our stop here to coincide with the large Masai market that it seemed sold everything imaginable, including Masai cattle. Second, I was going to ride a camel, an item from the 'bucket list'.

The Masai weekly market was a short distance outside our campsite, and spread itself at some length along both sides of the main road. Here vendors would bring an immense variety of wares to be sold, or locals set blankets or tarps on the ground and stacked up various fruits, vegetables, cooked items or crafts. A few nearby tiny canteens or outdoor bars became social gathering places as well, but the majority of activity took place out in the open sunshine.

The market was a place where a local woman might get her hair braided or even nails done while sitting on a stool, or have a colourful dress made. A few makeshift kiosks of boards and tarps were set up. Clusters of goods were piled on the ground, on the occasional table or rickety stand, or displayed on upright pieces of cardboard. Sometimes the wares were shaded by a large, beach-style umbrella. In all, it was a fascinating, noisy and bustling place as I wandered among the overwhelming variety of goods: stacks of new pots and pans; sacks of something piled everywhere; tomatoes piled in pyramids; maize; potatoes and onions; sandals and shoes stacked in various piles; woman's garments; underwear and enormous bras; a few blouses suspended on hangars on a pole; t-shirts; simple toys; sunglasses; pictures and postcards ... it was in fact a dream world for the addict of garage sales, bargain basements and liquidation outlets. Combine all this with the intense colour of all the bright blankets and wraps that everyone wore, and you would think you were at a circus or a festival. Not only did I see a phantasmagoria of colour and activity, but I could as well touch, taste, smell and feel the market. Everyone seemed to be talking in Swahili at once. If they weren't socializing or selling, they were bargaining for a best price.

Set somewhat away from the hub of the vendor's market were permanent fences and corrals where the coveted Masai cattle were sold. This was obviously the focus for many of the men at the market, who were gathered here in throngs. Although the breed of cattle was similar to those types of bovine most suited to the climate and preferred by the Masai, there were otherwise cattle of every shape, size and colour. Many had the large horns we have come to associate with the Masai. Outside of the activity going on in the corrals, large bulls or cows with calves were standing with their owners in a large dusty area where potential buyers were inspecting them. In one of the corrals, a man was painting figures on the sides of cattle with a stick. In broken English spoken by an affable Masai teen, I was told that this was to identify the cattle, although I could not understand whether it was the identification of the buyer or seller. The Masai men in the cattle compound were also dressed in bright colours and blankets, and were usually holding a walking stick. An artist would see this scene as a complete canvas of color, equal to that of the vendors market. At this site there were not only hundreds of cattle, but also hundreds of Masai men as well. Several cattle were restrained with a rope attached to a large ring in its nose. Occasionally I would see an animal decide not to go where it was intended, and was entertained by seeing the owner, often with his sons, running after it. Perhaps the runaway cow was more aware than I of what was taking place here, for I was told by one of our own safari group that had also been attracted to the cattle market as a place of interest, that the sale of cattle here was primarily for slaughter.

Among this busy crowd of men and animals I wandered as a visible minority, but my presence in general was tolerated and I did not feel unwelcome. In fact, in both markets I received several waves, nods of acknowledgement or friendly shouts of "Jambo mzungu" (hello whiteman), "Habri Yako"(what's up with you), "Mambo"(how's things), or just a plain "Karibu"(welcome). What distinguished this market as a whole from many of the others we had visited was that there were few hockers here trying to aggressively peddle their wares... just ordinary, every day people.

On my way out of the market I was drawn to the sound of rap music from a mobile stage that was situated on the back of a large transport truck. A group of rappers were singing, dancing and lip-synching to some loud music projected through two huge speakers. A crowd of Masai had gathered, and some seemed familiar with the performing group. I was told that these were the winners from a contest sponsored by Vodocom, a cell phone company, and as winners they were performing in villages, on tour. I thought perhaps they were a version of 'African Idol'. Having just wandered through an ageless, traditional village market, at the very least I assessed the stage performance to be rather a blatant but interesting juxtaposition. With this thought, I went to find my camel.

Masai Cattle Market

Although I knew I was succumbing to a tourist's embellishment, the three camels that were feeding outside our campsite had caught my attention when we first arrived. I had heard others tell me of their experience riding on a camel, and about how unique it was. Although I grew up on a farm with horses, and as a kid was accustomed to riding, I knew this would be different. I had to give it a try, and in fact felt a little giddy at being a kid again.

When I reported to the camel master, he motioned me to a tawny brown, standing camel that looked at me with what I thought was a rather vexed expression. After all, I was disturbing his feeding and it was quite hot for a ride. However, with the owners instruction the camel condescended to lower itself to the ground, its front legs folding up under its body. I thought that every part of the camel must have decided to go to the ground independently, for it was not a smooth descent but rather a series of wobbly, jerky motions that with effort finally got it to the earth. Even while it squatted there, I was surprised at how tall it still appeared, and it took more effort than I had suspected to seat myself in the camel saddle that had been provided. It was not like sitting upright in a horse saddle by any means, and I found myself leaning at a sharp angle forward, knees pressed tight against the camel to keep me from falling straight ahead.

If I thought the camel was awkward getting down, getting up was an even greater complication. As it began to move those independent parts to raise itself, I was tossed and moved around in swinging motions that in the end pretty well covered the compass. But with the camel finally standing, I was able to sit a bit more upright, and I became a little more comfortable. I was pleased that the camel seemed well kept, and even felt a little guilty for taking it for a walk in the heat of the day. But then I realized it was far more acclimatized than I, and off we went in a rocking, swaying, ambulatory motion that moved half my body forward, and then backward, with each alternating step. The only problem now was that neither halves of my moving body were in sync with the other. I felt it was not unlike when I had been tossed around in the jeep on our bumpy ride in the Ngorongoro crater. However, by the time we got to our turn around point, I had somewhat got the hang of it, and began to enjoy the experience of camel riding in Africa. Somehow however, the fantasy of wandering the dunes in the Sahara did not quite match the reality of riding my camel next to the Masai cattle market, but for now it would have to do.

I actually found that from the height of the camel, I had a great view of the activity over in the nearby cattle market, where the colourful blankets of the Masai stood out. The more distant scenery was also striking, with two mountains rising skyward in the distance. The furthest mountain appeared a faint, hazy blue outline with a misty swash of white barely visible on its peak. Then, with some surprise, I recognized that it was Mount Kilimanjaro ... now being viewed from the back of a camel.

To The Highlands Of Loshoto
Cameras on Kili; Lofty Loshoto

Safari Days 19-20

Cameras On Kili

My alarm watch beeped at 5:20 in the morning, and before leaving the tent I engaged in my morning safari routine: slipping the sleeping bag into its nylon protector; stuffing the mosquito net into its pouch; arranging what articles would be needed for the day's activities into the daypack; folding other belongings into my camp bag; and finally dressing. Because it was still dark, all this was accomplished in the spotlight of my small halogen headlamp. Next would be a wash-up before that first cup of rich African coffee that Nick and John always had ready over the camp coals. The remaining job before breakfast was to break down the tent, fold and roll it into its pack, and carry all the items, including my foam mattress and pillow, to the safari truck for loading.

Everyone was well organized for the day, and *JuJu* rolled out on the main two-lane highway in good time. We would be traveling back through Arushu, head west to Moshi, then turn south at some point to our final destination of Loshoto, high in the Mountains off the Rift Valley. I was especially excited to be going to Moshi, because it was from here I would get a close look at Mount Kilimanjaro. However, since Kili can create its own weather on the mountain, and the peak is often shrouded in mist or cloud, that good look could equally depend on some good luck. But for now it was a beautiful, sunny day with a clear sky and I was optimistic about the prospects.

Even though Arushu is by comparison a town more affluent than most we had visited to date, I was also equally impressed with the quality of buildings as we got closer to Moshi. No doubt this was influenced by the fact that Kilimanjaro is renowned as a tourist and trekking destination. Additionally, the countryside is also quite lush as compared to the arid areas east of Arushu, and the increase in precipitation here has meant an increase in agriculture. Banana trees were frequent, and around Moshi gum and other planted trees formed attractive boulevards.

The distant Kilimanjaro continued to enlarge as we traveled towards it. However, the sun was rising from the opposite side, and the smoky-blue apparition we were seeing was not the crisp view I wanted in the frame of my camera. Although the day was brightening, there was also a swash of white forming on the east side of Kili, and I became further concerned I may not get the view for which I longed. And then, there it was ... in all its magnificence and splendor ... as clear as one would wish to see ... the snows of Kilimanjaro. Karoma may have seen me hanging out the open flaps of *JuJu* for the past few kilometres, while trying to capture the pinnacle in my lens, for we suddenly veered into a pullout and stopped to soak in the beauty of Kili's contours. Near us was a maize field, which when framed with the mountain, offered a wonderfully unique perspective. Tasha informed us that although they have traveled past Kili many times, this was one of the clearest views they have ever seen of the mountain.

Lofty Loshoto

Leaving Kili behind, we traveled in a southeasterly direction, again following the Rift Valley. We were making a noticeable transition from where the indigenous Masai thrived mainly on cattle and livestock, to where their livelihood was now primarily growing crops. As a result, gone from the landscape were the multitude of cattle and goat herds seen grazing by the side of the road. Now we saw vast maize fields, and past the village of Mwanga were endless fields of pineapples. I could detect a more noticeable Muslim presence. Village mosques were more frequent and an increasing number of men were wearing the pillbox-shaped cap. More women were wearing burkas. Sanskrit writing began to appear on signs, and on the front of some buses appeared the slogan 'Glory To God'.

About four and a half hours after having left our campsite near Arushu, we turned off the main road at a village called Mombo, and started winding up a very steep valley to our destination at Loshoto. This scenic village is perched near the top of the climb, in the Usambra Mountains. The ascent proved to be an adventure in itself, as we clawed our way around endless hairpin curves. Here the road's edge seemed only stomach-wrenching metres away from a free-fall drop into the dizzying valley below. The problem was not only in going up, but the seemingly out-of-control traffic of packed buses, trucks or other vehicles sailing down at incredible speeds. The narrow road appeared to have only inches for passing. There were similarities in this turning and tossing ascent up the mountain, to the extreme white water raft ride that four of us had taken. We started calling out rafting commands, "Lean in"... "Lean left"... "Lean right" ... "Get down"" ... Hang on". We added one more ... "Close you eyes!".

If you were brave enough to leave your eyes open, the scenery was astounding. When the fear of the slow-grinding climb with its near misses was mastered, one noticed things like the blue gum trees planted on the outer edge of the road, also functioning as a guardrail. Small waterfalls tumbled intermittently from the rivulet that carved its way down through the deep valley. The soil was an ochre red in colour, not unlike at Jinja, and appeared extremely fertile in its support of both natural and cultivated vegetation. Tiny etched-out fields and terraces balanced at forty-five degree angles as they clung to the mountainsides. It was as if we had entered a totally different world from anything we had seen to date in Africa. With such beauty, and the exhilaration we felt in being here, it was obvious why Tasha and Karoma had included this unique area on the safari itinerary.

At one point of the climb we encountered a large truck incredulously over-crammed with countless passengers, all jammed into its back wooden-framed box. This scene, which amazed us at first, became quite common. That so many people could squeeze their bodies into that amount of space seemed to defy the laws of physics. However, Karoma informed us that having often traveled African-style like this, it is not the getting in which is the biggest problem, but getting out. He said that when you arrived at your destination, your body was numb from the waist down.

Just before the village of Loshoto, we finally turned off the road and onto a driveway that wound up to the Lawns Hotel, our accommodation for the night. Although always comfortable in my tent, I was looking forward to the break, and particularly to having a room that included a bathroom with a shower. Most of the rooms had views overlooking a forested valley, and Loshoto village was only a ten to fifteen minute walk away. Here would also be a good time to catch up on making some entries into my travelogue. At this point, I knew our safari was shifting its focus from the viewing of wildlife in the reserves and parks, to more exposure to the cultures and customs of the areas we would now be visiting.

With an open agenda, in the morning I wandered down the packed dirt driveway of the hotel and along the main road into the village of Loshoto. Turning onto the main road, there was the usual traffic of pedestrians I had come to expect in Africa. Passing by a group of men and women who were using machetes to clear brush from the side of the road, I entered into the busy village. I discovered it had a market.

The market was situated on a relatively flat area, with steep inclines rising on all sides a short distance away. What at first seemed like just a couple of streets of kiosks and stalls, in fact became a maze of alleyways where hundreds of marketers bartered for goods or were selling them. Items of every conceivable nature were sold in small shops attached to one another, or from single stalls. Other merchandise, including fruits and vegetables, were simply spread out on the ground on some sacking or tarp. What was refreshing here was that there was an absence of hockers harassing you to buy their products. I felt comfortable wandering around, and squeezed past people to explore narrow streets and out-of-the way alleys. It was impossible not to appreciate the setting, where on the perimeter of the market banana plants and other vegetation combined to blanket the surrounding mountains.

Having rested a bit after overdosing on Loshoto's mountain market, in the afternoon I set out with another member from our group to explore a switchback road that ascended high above the valley. Since so much travel is done on foot, there was considerable pedestrian traffic on the road. This included many students in their school uniforms who were walking to their homes, back up the mountain, as well as a substantial number of women returning from the market with enormous loads balanced on their heads. As we hiked along, eventually what was a very bumpy, paved road became an even bumpier unpaved road, but we continued ascending while enjoying the wonderful vistas of the slowly disappearing valley below. The crops that were planted on the steep slopes surrounding us were primarily a mixture of banana trees, vegetables, sugar cane, even some coffee plants. The crops were intermingled with other larger trees to prevent soil erosion on the steep banks.

Still up we went, climbing higher, always wondering what was around the next corner and wondering how far we were from the top of the mountain. We found ourselves beginning to traverse sharp, small valleys, as the road passed through an interconnection of v-shaped depressions. Here the road was filled with ruts from previous rainstorms. At one point we were able to look far beyond to another range of mountains, and even further we were able to detect the blue-gray smudge of the Rift Valley itself. Although we often received greetings of "Jambo" (hello), many were confused to see two wandering mzungus this high up the mountain.

After nearly two hours of uninterrupted hiking, we reached a small village at the top and walked along the only main dirt street that had a few clapboard, solitary shops. Even here commerce was alive and well. An elderly woman was selling tomatoes she had piled high on a sack, spread on the ground. Several young men were standing at a tiny bicycle repair shop. However, no sooner had we finally reached the top when we noticed that the light was starting to fade. We knew we had better start our descent quickly, before it became too dark to travel the rut-filled road.

As we made our way down, we were surprised to still see all the pedestrian traffic walking towards us from the other direction. Women, with loads on their heads, were still returning from the market. Students were still coming home from school. Even though it was already beginning to get dark, it would be darker still when these people arrived back at their homes, and it was likely that early the next morning they would be walking back down the mountain again to the village. It was not an easy lifestyle.

Onto The Indian Ocean
*A Long Shortcut to Bagamoya; Lay Down Your Heart;
Sunrise Beach; The Luggage Cart to Dar Es Salaam*

Safari Days 21-23

A Long Shortcut to Bagamoya
I awoke at 5:00 am to the sound of loudspeakers calling the villagers to the mosque for morning prayers. We had over 400 kilometres to travel to Bagamoya, situated on the Indian Ocean, and after breakfast *JuJu* started snaking back down the mountain to the Rift Valley. On our way to Loshoto, two days earlier we had passed large fields of pineapples. Now traveling eastward again along the valley, I saw similar plants. However, the ones here were enormous, and I foolishly commented that I had never seen three-foot pineapples before. Somewhat embarrassed I was informed that the plants were called sisal, and were used in making braided rope. In the market in Loshoto I had seen massive coils of the rope at several stalls, and now understood why it was such a common commodity in the area. Fields of sisal seemed to stretch into the vastness of the valley.

Eventually these fields gave way to other types of agriculture, now influenced by the increasing proximity to the Indian Ocean. Maize, banana and pineapples became intermingled with coconut palms, and citrus trees began to appear in small groves. The markets were full of these products, both in the stalls and in piles of fruit and vegetables stacked on the ground near them. Also typical of most of the East African markets we had seen, the markets here were also both bustling commercial centres as well as social gathering areas.

At one of our stops Karoma was told that there were construction road delays en route to Dar Es Salaam, which was the route we were taking before going north to Bagamoya. He was also told there was a shortcut that avoided these delays, and that it completely bypassed the busy city of Dar Es Salaam. Apparently it would only take about half an hour. Judging this to be a good alternative, off we went onto a rural back-road. It was a fascinating drive that allowed us to see how simply the locals in this area lived. We observed that for the most part they had a meager existence, yet as we passed by their basic shelters or villages there were enthusiastic waves and much excitement. After all, it was not every day they would see driving by their homes a huge, green safari truck with several Mzungus staring out the side flaps, and waving back. For the most part, the huts and hovels we saw were either built by the side of the road and in clearings, or were partially buried in the forest.

The dirt road we traveled had several places where Karoma had to gear down to cross small log bridges, or drive through dips and depressions in the road. Our half-hour short cut was expanding into a much longer interval, and soon we had clocked over two hours. However, no one in our layed-back group seemed to mind, for in taking this off-road route we understood we had actually been given a rare glimpse into both the geography and lifestyle of a rarely visited area. The unplanned detour became another one of those inadvertent and unexpected stolen moments enhancing our travel, and it had enriched our day.

Literally breaking out of the countryside, we found we had arrived at a town that sported a fairly busy market, with many brick or clapboard businesses. After driving through the main section of town, with its onlookers waving or staring as we went by, I caught a glimpse of a sparkling, green horizon for a brief second. Suddenly ... there it was. We had literally been dumped out of the Tanzanian backcountry and hinterland to be plunked onto the beaches of the Indian Ocean. We had arrived at our beach resort, nestled among a multitude of coconut palms with a large swimming pool nearby. It was only a couple of minutes walk from the campsite to the resort beach which had a bar and restaurant looking directly onto the azure ocean. Our safari now officially transformed from African beasts to African beaches. I kicked off my sandals as I crossed the white powdery sand to dip my feet in the waters of the Indian Ocean for the very first time.

Lay Down Your Heart
We were in Bagamoya, a most beautiful setting, but one strangely juxtaposed with its black mark on history. Bagamoya was a holding market for slaves seized from the interior of Africa. From here, dhows transported the captured labourers across to the Island of Zanzibar, then onto other locations using slave labour. A popular destination for the slaves was Arabia itself. They were also sent to work on spice plantations on other islands. The slaves were brought to Bagamoya in chains, mostly by Arab slave traders, who imprisoned them in atrocious conditions until they could be shipped off.

Besides enjoying the beaches and beauty of Bagamoya, I wandered through the old, historic part of town where its buildings, although deteriorating, truly reflected the deep roots this area had as an early commercial centre, even apart from the slaves. Many safaris heading west into the interior would engage up to 130 porters to carry trade goods, equipment, supplies and ammunition. They originated and ended at this location, contributing to its busy commerce at the time. However, there is no doubt it was the slave trade that was the focus, and its old stone buildings could tell haunting tales. By the time the slaves had been brought to this destination, it was realized there was no longer any hope of escape. Enslavement for the rest of their lives was inevitable. Bagamoya literally means 'Lay Down Your Heart', and the name truly captures the despair felt by the slaves brought here.

Much of the morning was immersed in exploring Bagamoya and its history, including the role the Catholic Church played in the care and eventual emancipation of the slaves. However, by the time we returned to our campsite for lunch, I felt the lure of the ocean. In the afternoon I set out by myself to explore the beautiful beach, walking barefoot on the sand past fishing boats, past a large, busy local market, and past mangroves with acres of coconut groves nearby. Later in the evening I returned again to the beach to soak up the intoxicating view of the fishing dhows returning to the village at the end of the day. I eventually found myself focusing on the silhouette of a distant black sail that had been captured in the fiery, reflective trail of the sinking sun.

Sunrise Beach

In the morning we left Bagamoya and circumnavigated the larger city of Dar Es Salaam to arrive at another special location on the Indian Ocean. Our destination was Sunset Beach. Here we discovered that the long, curving beach which is washed by the blue-green waters of the Indian Ocean, is nothing but spectacular. Our accommodations were large tents permanently erected under thatched-roofed covers with pole supports. The large mosquito-netted doors of these special tents allowed one to gaze out onto the wonderful scenery. At this latter stage in our safari, the whole point of this location was simply to enjoy the day without any planned agendas before we would fly the next day from nearby Dar Es Salaam to the Island of Zanzibar. I settled in to enjoy a relaxing Safari beer or two, but in lieu of pink elephants I became a bit concerned when I thought I saw a camel come walking by on the beach.

Sunrise Beach has been appropriately named. Here the rising sun continues to change in colour, tones and hues while transforming the palm trees, dhows, thatched roofs and small fishing boats into distinct black silhouettes.

The Luggage Cart to Dar Es Salaam

With so much time spent in our safari truck, it did not seem possible that we were boarding *JuJu* for the last time. We were going to be taking a brief ferry ride across a small port bay to the downtown side of Dar Es Salaam, where an awaiting bus would transport us to the airport for a twenty-five minute flight to Zanzibar. When we stopped near the ferry terminal, Karoma flagged down the owner of a two-wheeled, rubber-tired pull cart to transport all of our luggage onto the ferry.

By the time we loaded the mounds of backpacks, duffle bags, suitcases and packages of souvenirs, the overloaded cart looked as if it would be impossible to move. However, the muscled Tanzanian cart-driver and his partner had carefully balanced the load to rest over the tires, and he quite effortlessly picked up the cart handles and set the cart in motion. Throngs of people were crowded on the street as the cart advanced toward the ferry terminal, with me at the side of the cart. The road, which had a slight decline, caused the heavy cart to speed up and soon the driver and his partner were awkwardly running to try to keep it from getting out of control. People were scattering everywhere, trying to avoid being rammed with a runaway cart. Tasha saw what was happening and immediately became concerned that the cart was distancing itself from the group, and that the luggage would therefore be no longer secure under our supervision. She yelled at me, "Dennis ... stay with the cart. Don't let it out of your sight!". I had just been designated to guard our luggage, and I did not want to disappoint.

Being in charge of the luggage turned out to be more challenging than I anticipated. First, the cart duo was now not only going at a good clip, but the cart was weaving in and out of the heavy traffic of vehicles and pedestrians, and I struggled to keep up with the erratic pattern. Second, my speed was handicapped by my loose sandals and by my heavy backpack, which I still shouldered. I finally managed to grab onto one of the packs on the cart, and was able to keep up by being pulled along with the load. We finally stopped at a terminal gate where they allowed only vehicles (and carts), into a paddock to await the ferry. I simply pretended I was one of the porters, although being a very visible Mzungu, the absurdity of that pretense did strike me later. However, I was allowed to pass through the barrier gate without having to present a ferry ticket that I did not yet have. Meanwhile, the rest of the group were directed through the pedestrian entrance and herded into a large caged area that was the holding room for the waiting passengers.

Within minutes of our arrival a blue, partially-painted, open-decked ferry docked. Like an invasion, the disembarking ferry passengers, carts, and occasional vehicle spilled out onto the grimy walkway and charged 'en mass' up the ramp, and past us. Simultaneously, the doors to the cage of waiting passengers opened to allow them to board the ferry. It was mass chaos, as those at the front started running madly and became integrated with the slower passengers who were still trying to get off the ferry. It was at that point that the two hired cart-pullers also tried to head for the ferry. They had already been paid and wanted to get to the other side at the front of the line so they could get rid of this load and be the first cart available for a new customer.

"No ... wait until the boss comes", I projected in my most authoritative voice, knowing Karoma was yet to return from having taken the safari truck to its mainland storage location.
"Time is money", came the response. "We go now!"

By this time I had already grabbed hold of the cart with one hand, was hanging onto some luggage with the other, and had my foot wedged under one of the tires. I told them again to wait for the boss. They hesitated, and I tried to explain why we had to wait, but all I got were glares and gestures feigning they did not understand. I was not to be fooled, for I assessed the usage of the expression 'time is money' indicated a pretty good understanding of the English language. In the end, they very reluctantly waited for two ferries, and when Karoma arrived he joined us in pushing the cart onto the ferry. As we approached the other side of the bay, I then realized the cart had now to be pushed up a steep hill to get it off the ferry. It would be difficult for the two cart pullers to do this on their own. Karoma understood this as well, and without hesitancy we both joined forces to push the cart to the area where the waiting bus was parked. Relieved that we had helped, the previously disgruntled cart puller turned to me, grinned and said, "Hakuna Mattata" (no worries). I too felt relieved that I was not leaving Dar Es Salaam having antagonized a cart puller, which I believed was not a very positive safari thing to do.

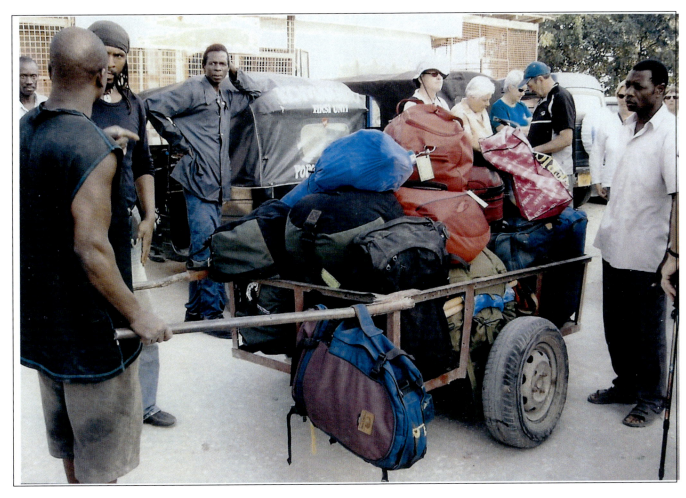

Picture by Maureen & Allan Jones

Zanzibar
Sauntering in Stonetown; Kendwa Rocks; Six Masai and a Canadian at Sea

Safari Days 24-27

Sauntering in Stonetown

Our twenty-five minute flight from the domestic airport at Dar across the water to the Island of Zanzibar was on a sixteen-passenger plane with Coastal Air. From the airport at Zanzibar we were bussed into Stonetown, fittingly named because of its impressive stone buildings jammed along very narrow streets. The historic buildings are made of the same coral stone from which the island itself is composed. Like Bagamoya, Stonetown's history is steeped in the slave trade. It was from here that the slaves imported from Bagamoya were dispersed to other locations.

The narrow streets of Stonetown are a maze of branching and interconnected passageways where it is easy to become disoriented. Most people meandering around the streets sooner or later become confused or lost, and therefore after settling into the Safari Lodge, Tasha took us on a practice run of how to get to and from our hotel.

One of the unique features of the buildings in Stonetown is the huge, intricately carved wood doors that highlight the entrances. The doors often have brass or iron knobs set into them, which apparently has origins back to a time in India when the knobs or spikes discouraged elephants from leaning against them. I spent the entire afternoon sauntering around the central area, rummaging through markets and shops, doing some banking and attempting to send some e-mail. My first attempt at e-mail was a 'deja vu' of the other unsuccessful attempts I had made while in Africa, in this case the system crashing before I could send it. I was also anxious to try some of the small restaurants that were either located near or on the beach, or tucked away in corners and back streets. My sense of adventure also compelled me to eat at the food stalls found primarily in one main market street. It was usually in full swing by early evening. Stonetown, with its disparate cultures of Africa, India, Arabia and Europe, became for me a unique place to play tourist for a couple of days. Getting lost became part of the entertainment.

The second evening in Stonetown I returned to a little Zanzibar restaurant where I had also lunched the previous day. Upon entering, I first gazed at the inviting and brightly painted room with its quilt-like wall hangings. I then noticed two women seated in the back area at a circular tiled bench, playing a game I had not seen before. The game was played from a carved wooden box in which coffee beans were being moved in and out of circular carved depressions or cups. I found out later the game is called Bao, and is known as the centuries old game that takes minutes to learn ... and a lifetime to master. For me, this all added to the ambiance and mystique of the small restaurant, enhanced also by the Muslim influence seen in its traditional designs and decorations.

From the menu I ordered what was in essence a lamb and vegetable turnover, infused with a wonderful blend of local spices, including cardamom. I also ordered an aromatic blend of Zanzibar mixed spice-tea that was served in a unique coconut shell teapot. Since Zanzibar is often referred to as the 'Spice Island', I had already visited a local plantation where, in an outdoor clearing, I sampled a variety of such teas. I was anxious to try this special house blend, and was not disappointed.

After my meal I made my way back through the maze of passageways to my hotel. Along the way I passed a number of women dressed in their black burkas, and took note of the men returning from the mosque, dressed in their immaculate white gowns. It was an early night, for tomorrow we would be leaving by bus to Kendwa Rocks, another beach resort at the north end of the island.

Kendwa Rocks

In the morning, our self-serve breakfast was waiting for us on the rooftop patio of the hotel, several flights up from the lobby. Here, sipping on my morning coffee, I absorbed a unique view of Stonetown as I overlooked the corrugated tin and metal roofs all jammed together. Like the buildings themselves, many of the rooftops also showed signs of deterioration. We were approaching the last two or three days of our wonderful adventure together, and as there were various departure times for our return trips, the beach resort at Kendwa Rocks would be the last destination where we would all be together as a group. We would have spent twenty-eight days on safari in each other's company, bonding and forming friendships, so parting we knew would be a significant event. I had decided to spend an extra day on the beach, and would return for an additional day in Stonetown before beginning my two-day, five-flights journey back to British Columbia.

Leaving the Safari Lodge was somewhat of an event in itself, since the streets were too narrow for a vehicle, and it was necessary to walk to where a minibus awaited us on the outskirts of the central maze. Loaded down with backpacks and luggage and walking almost in single file to be able to navigate the slim passageways, our group of mzungus trudged the short distance through the thread-like streets. It became apparent for some reason that most of the locals associated walking with your backpacks as an arrival event, not a departing one. As a result, from dim shadows that peered out from the darkness of the wood-carved doorways, we kept hearing "Karibu" (welcome). I jokingly commented that I thought they anticipated we would be spending more money".

When we arrived at our minibus, we realized that getting all the luggage through the very narrow aisle of the vehicle would be a major job. The problem was solved by sliding open one of the back windows, and passing the bulky bundles through the open space. By the time the luggage was in, and we had squished into the remaining available space including sitting on fold-down aisle seats, it seemed as if the multiple bodies in the bus had melded into one. To some good-natured banter about our seating intimacy, off we went.

We traveled along the main road heading to the northwest point of Zanzibar Island, passing a multitude of coconut palms, banana trees and spice plantations. The paved road is very good by African standards, that is until we turned off onto a side-road leading to Kendwa Rocks. It revived memories of the bumpy dirt roads we had already traversed to gain access to many of the exotic and out-of-the-way places we visited across East Africa. But the side-road was not a lengthy journey, and soon we found ourselves at Sunset Beach Lodge, situated on a wide, sandy promontory jutting out into the Indian Ocean. The magnificent mocha-coloured beach, itself, stretches for about 3 or 4 kilometres and shares several resorts. Besides being a popular tourist destination, I met a number of people for whom Kendwa Rocks was a starting point, mid-point or final destination for their own safaris. Some had also integrated the visit into their Mount Kilimanjaro climb itineraries.

Settling into bungalow #37, it did not take me long to get back into African beach mode, and to slip into my beach shorts and sandals. I was impressed with the large four-posted bed in my room, all enclosed in a mosquito net. From it I could see out of a large picture window onto a beach courtyard full of palm trees. A two-minute walk away was a thatched-roofed restaurant and bar that offered a panorama of the entire beach bay and the emerald-hued ocean. The area was advertised on our safari itinerary as a place to relax, with options of diving, snorkeling, swimming or sailing in a dhow. However, after the exciting but intense pace of the past 26 days, doing nothing but beaching seemed to appeal to me most for the moment. The time spent on the beach seemed to evaporate. For the first two days I did nothing but suntan, walk on the beach, play beach volleyball, eat meals of cold Zanzibar octopus salads for lunch and curried Zanzibar seafood for suppers, and enjoy a diet of Tusker, Safari or Kilimanjaro beers. However, after having satiated myself on food and drink, on the third morning I was ready, and in need of, an extended trek. The next day I planned to hike back to the main paved road by which we had come, and down to a fishing village a few kilometres away. From there I would return in a circular route by walking back along the shore, knowing I would have to negotiate past a promontory that stretched a short distance out into the water.

Six Masai and a Canadian at Sea

My first task in the morning before my hike was to say goodbye to most of my safari mates who were leaving Kendwa Rocks to return to Stonetown airport to fly back to Dar Es Salaam, then onto their homes in Australia or New Zealand. Managing to keep my composure amidst the nostalgia of being so close together for the past twenty-eight days or so, I saw my new friends off, then headed down the dirt road to find the fishing village. By the time I had taken a number of detours exploring various trails branching off to other beach resorts or unknown locations, it was over two hours before I meandered among the coral-stone huts of the fishing village to find the ocean again. On the beach I passed a few boys in bare feet who were playing soccer with an old deflated ball, and then wove among clusters of traditional fishing crafts to start my return journey back along the shore. Fishermen were organizing for their next outing, tending to their nets or boats. I noticed that the tide was considerably higher than when I had left earlier in the morning, and began to wonder if it would be possible to make it past the rocky, coral promontory I needed to circumnavigate. Otherwise I would have to return by my original route, which would take considerably longer.

I walked the beach for some distance, but it was becoming increasingly clear the tide was too high now to make it back along the shore, and I was running out of options. Having done a few Ironman distance swims in triathlons, I did have the alternative of swimming out around the rocky promontory, but was not comfortable swimming where I might encounter an undertow. Since I was now in an area of multiple resorts scattered along the beach, I wondered if there might be a water taxi service of some kind that could transport me back. It was then I saw a rather unusual sight, and it triggered the idea of trying to hitch hike back to my beach.

Six young Masai in their traditional dress, as I had seen them on the Masai Mara, were trying to climb into a large, old plank boat. I noticed the craft had the name 'Spanish Dancer' written on the side. With their attempts at trying to board the rocking boat that was bobbing up, down and sideways in the waves, it was obvious they were not of the ocean and not comfortable in this element. I guessed that they must be trying to get a ride somewhere, and thought the boat might possibly be going in the same direction I was heading ... back to Kendwa Rocks. I ran up to where the commotion was taking place and started asking if they were going my way.

No one spoke English, but one Masai motioned me to a young white woman who seemed to be in charge, and I asked again. The large plank boat was already moving out to sea. She nodded when I mentioned Kendwa Rocks, and in a strong accent she yelled over the sound of the breaking waves, "Climb in!". By this time the water was more than waist high, and my efforts to clamor over the boat's steep side reminded me of trying to get back into the raft in the turbulent waters of the Nile back at Bujegali Falls. The last of the Masai to board the craft had fared no better than I, but we finally all managed to get into the boat. Once in the craft, I glanced up and found myself among a brood of wide-eyed, excited and loudly chattering Masai who were obviously quite uncomfortable with the bobbing and rocking motion of the old craft in the surf. I felt pleased, however, that I could now just relax and be transported back to my beach, where at the restaurant I planned to enjoy another octopus salad with a beer. However, my intended simple boat ride did not transpire in that manner, and at about fifty metres off shore we slowed, and pulled alongside a similar empty boat that bobbed and tossed even more aggressively in the heavier surf. It became clear we were expected to change boats at this point.

After my many nights on safari, and in campsites being guarded by hippo and hyena chasing Masai, I now regarded the Masai as brave warriors. I could not help, however, but be very amused at the challenge these young Masai men of the plains now faced. They had to jump from one tossing boat to another, complicated by the problem that the movement of both vessels was completely out of sync. When one boat went up, the other went down, and with every other wave, the boats parted. If the jump were mistimed, the consequence would be that a body would end up in the deep, wavy water. I was quite certain from observing their behaviour, that none of the Masai could swim.

My six new acquaintances all began pointing at the other boat, and began chattering at once, then pointing to the boat again. Obviously no one wanted to go first. Finally, they began rehearsing for the jump with dips of body movement and the swinging of arms to assist with the motion. Eventually with much commotion, they all were safely boarded. I then quickly made the jump across, but I was still laughing when I landed in the boat. There were some curious stares. At that point they must have realized what I found so humorous, for all of a sudden all six of them burst into laughter and pointed at me enjoying myself. I could then hear the teasing in their voices as they slapped each other on the back or shoulders, and repeatedly recreated the jump with their hands.

I felt fortunate to have hitched a ride with a boat that included these lads. On the one hand they seemed so out of place on the beach and in the boat, yet on the other hand I knew how competent and comfortable they were back home in their own challenging environment. Despite their widening eyes each time a rogue wave hit the side of the boat, causing them to grab wildly at whatever was available, they had a great sense of humour and enjoyed each others' company. When we arrived at the beach at Kendwa rocks, there were mysterious looks from nearby sunbathers as six colourfully blanketed Masai, adorned in their striking hoops and jewelry, jumped into the shallow water from the boat ... that is, six Masai and one white Canadian mzungu ... who together had shared an adventure at sea.

The Last Safari Sunset
Conclusion

Reluctantly it was time to leave the beach and begin the two-day series of travel legs that would eventually get me back home. The first transport was by minibus that took me from Kendwa Rocks for a last night back in Stonetown. After returning to the Safari Lodge hotel where our group had previously stayed, I once again meandered through the tunnel-like streets. I now knew, however, that when I heard from behind me the repetitive tinkle from a bicycle bell, or a sharp beep from a scooter, I should casually press close to a wall to give enough space for passing. I found that I could now do this without looking back or even breaking stride.

When I reviewed my itinerary for my return home, I realized that in booking my flights from Stonetown to Dar Es Salaam (with a connecting flight returning to Entebbe), I had not at that time understood the need to also factor in the concept of 'Africa Time'. Africa Time is where things run on an independent schedule all its own, regardless of any planned or organized agenda. My morning flight arriving from Stonetown to Dar only left me fifty minutes to change airlines for my next flight to Entebbe, a very marginal time when in Africa. Having by now learned a great deal about the need here to be prepared for any contingency where the acronyms AWA and TIA are rule of thumb ('Africa Wins Again', and 'This Is Africa'), I decided I needed to leave Stonetown the next morning at an earlier time, just to be safe. Unfortunately there were no earlier flights with Precision Air with which I had originally booked, so even without a refund I still decided to purchase a separate ticket with Coastal Aviation. This would give me twenty more minutes to make my transfer. After several attempts elsewhere, I finally located a tiny back-street travel office that would handle my booking, but between faxes and telephone calls it took over three hours to complete the transaction. In the end it turned out to be a very prudent decision, as I found out later that Precision Air at the last minute decided not to fly at the time as scheduled, and I would have missed my only connecting flight.

Finally resolving my flight dilemma and completing some last minute shopping, the realization that my whole, incredible adventure in East Africa was now at a close began to impact me. It had all been such a positive experience, and I decided that I should spend the last lingering moments indulging in some simple, but meaningful gesture that for me acknowledged the significance of this journey. It had been a beautiful clear day, but soon the sun would be setting. I loved an African sunset. It did not take long to decide that my final time would be spent sipping a Tusker beer on the beach, and watching the sunset over the Indian Ocean, while reminiscing about many of the rich, stolen moments that had been part of this safari. I made my way down to a table in front of the Livingston Beach Hotel. The setting was perfect. Framed in my vista were a dozen or so wooden dhows that either were secured by ropes to the beach, or were gliding to and fro across the shimmering water. I marveled that the distinct wooden booms of these boats, angling diagonally across the hulls, have remained the same for centuries.

My beer arrived, and the first flavourful sip of the Tusker, with its cool effervescence, reminded me that it had been twenty-nine days ago that I had first sampled a refreshment with my new Kiwi and Aussie mates. I let my mind wander in an abandoned reminiscence, as the late afternoon light began to change ever so slightly- a promise of what was to come. I thought back to how excited I had been when I caught my first glimpse of Africa, as our plane banked above Entebbe in preparation for landing. I remembered boarding *JuJu* for the first time, and driving through the outskirts of Kampala, with its explosion of hectic markets and commerce, then on through Uganda.

Another sip of Tusker ... then came the rush of memories of white water rafting on the Nile at Jinja and Bujegali Falls. At one moment the Nile was uneventfully calm and peaceful, as we paddled its quiet open stretches of lake-like water. But we also discovered the ancient river could reveal an awesome power, overturning our raft and sucking us into its watery folds of froth ... leaving us choking, gasping, and pondering for milliseconds our possible demise. I sipped and smiled, remembering the dynamic tales told around the campfire that evening by the four rafting survivors from our group, each version becoming a bit more dramatic in its content, and seemingly more dangerous.

There was by now a slight peach colour to the sky, as the sun initiated a more quickening descent, which in turn gave darker hues to the dhows. My mind continued its reverie, processing events in a loose chronological order. Unconsciously at the same time I was also aware that a number of local boys and younger Zanzibar men were swimming or playing in the water nearby, but this faded away as I recalled the first time I gazed upon the Rift Valley, seeing it stretch endlessly in both directions, as I stood high above it. When we descended to the valley floor, we had followed along the arid plain to Lake Baringo. It was here that hippos had been chased from our campsite, and where I sat reading on a camp chair, just a few feet from a sunbathing croc with its gaping mouth open. From here we had also visited the remote Pokot nomads, learning that despite their survival-based environment and how simply they lived, they still exuded a special contentment and enjoyment of life as they clapped, sang and danced to the ringing rhythms of their bouncing bells.

The sun had significantly lowered. Like a peacock, it now radiated a plumage of yellow, orange and red in flamboyant preparation for its dramatic disappearance. My tusker bottle was empty, but I was not yet ready to leave before the final curtain. The waiter recommended a savannah cider, something I had not yet tried. As he left, I was already indulging in more safari reflections, recalling those rich days spent searching for game in the various parks and reserves. Lake Nakuru was an amazing compact park that allowed us to feast at close distances on the images of African buffalo, zebras, giraffes, impalas, gazelles and the mass of rhinos protected in its boundaries. Then there was the Masai Mara, with its magnificent elephants ... cows, bulls, young frisky calves. I could still feel the excitement as our hot air balloon just skimmed over the head-shaking, tusk-wielding young bull elephant that had been so vexed at our quiet, but sudden descent from the sky. In the Ngorongoro Crater I could have reached down and touched the shaggy mane of the unconcerned male lion that circled our vehicle. I had seen the lone, princely cheetah sitting up and scanning the horizon of his crater home. Then there was life on the safari truck itself, and in the campsites. I had the good fortune of being with a most wonderful community of people who also embraced the adventure, thereby enriching and enhancing it.

Watching the final vestiges of the fiery sun sink into the Indian Ocean, I realized that the entire last month on safari had seemed to me like suspended time. The routine of putting up the tent and taking it down, gathering together for meals, boarding and disembarking from *JuJu*, walking through markets and villages, observing and engaging in unique and different customs, all these became the flow of experiences within that suspended time. I now regarded them as the precious stolen moments that, blended together, had allowed me to touch Africa ... and to be touched by Africa in return. I glanced one last time at the glowing ember disappearing from the sky ... this last safari sunset.

ISBN 1-4251-8627-0

9 781425 186272